# LIFE OF A
# SAINT

### BY MICHAEL KURN

Best Wishes

First Published 2020

Copyright © Michael Kurn & Desire Dream Vision Ltd

No Part of this book may be reproduced in any form without permission from the author, publisher and Desire Dream Vision Ltd, except by a reviewer who may quote in a review. The interviews and artwork in the book are the © of Michael Kurn & Desire Dream Vision Limited

Desire Dream Vision Ltd Registration No : 10676192

## AUTHOR
**MICHAEL KURN**
WWW.MICHAELKURN.COM
Social Media @Michael Kurn

**MANAGED BY**
MACKENZIE WELLER MANAGEMENT
WWW.MACKENZIEWELLER.COM

ISBN : 978-1-83853-261-1

## WWW.LIFEOFASAINT.CO.UK
SOCIAL MEDIA: @LifeOfASaint85

A catalogue copy of this book is available in the British Library

**PUBLISHED BY**

**DESIRE DREAM VISION LTD**

# LIFE OF A
# SAINT

**LIFE OF A SAINT**

# ACKNOWLEDGEMENTS

A huge thank you to everyone who has made this book possible.

To all the players for their time in sharing their stories and for all the memories they have given us.

Special thanks also to Mike Thew who has helped no end with this book, without his help organising the interviews and his support this book wouldn't have been possible.

Thanks also Saints Archive and Saints World for their support.

# LIFE OF A SAINT

## DEDICATION

This book is dedicated to every fan who has ever stood in the terraces,
who has sung **"Oh When The Saints"** with pride
and has supported our great club through the highs and lows.

I also dedicate this book to every player who has worn the red and white.
You have taken us on some journey, provided us with stories
to tell future generations and given us endless memories.
For that we are all truly thankful.

**LIFE OF A SAINT**

LIFE OF A SAINT

# CONTENTS

FOREWORD - ONCE A SAINT ALWAYS A SAINT ... 11
LAWRIE McMENEMY ... 15
MATTHEW LE TISSIER ... 25
JIMMY CASE ... 39
JOHN SYDENHAM ... 47
TERRY PAINE ... 55
FRANCIS BENALI ... 65
PAUL JONES ... 75
JASON DODD ... 79
DAVID PRUTTON ... 89
MIKE EARLS ... 97
DANNY WALLACE ... 107
DENIS HOLLYWOOD ... 113
MANNY ANDRUSZEWSKI ... 119
BILL BEANEY ... 127
JAMES BEATTIE ... 133
DENNIS ROFE ... 141
DAVID PUCKETT ... 149
GLENN COCKERILL ... 159
RUEBEN AGBOOLA ... 165
ANDY COOK ... 171
JOS HOOIVELD ... 177
THE HOME OF A SAINT - THE DELL ...183

# LIFE OF A SAINT

## FOREWORD

# ONCE A SAINT ALWAYS A SAINT

Growing up all I ever wanted to do was to be in that number. It's a feeling so many of us will only ever dream of and only a small few will ever get to experience:

## "THE LIFE OF BEING A SAINT"

I think it is fair to say at some point in our lives growing up we all dreamed about pulling on those famous red and white stripes. Imagining what it would feel like lining up alongside our heroes and walking out in front of the Southampton faithful.

Growing up I remember playing football in the school playground at lunchtime, all my friends wanted to be Beckham or Ronaldo but not me though, I wanted to be a Saint; Le Tissier one day and Oakley the next. When I scored I didn't run off celebrating like Thierry Henry, I raised my arm aloft and ran around with my arm whirling just like Mick Channon.

You see I grew up a Saint. I grew up dreaming of legends past, Keegan, Ball, Stokes, and Shilton. Who needs Charlton and Best when you had Sydenham and Paine.

The Dell was my church and growing up I didn't get to go too often. Driving past I would gaze out of the car window imagining the match day roar.

When I did go though, it always felt like home and I was lucky enough to be there when we said goodbye. I saw with my own eyes the magic of Le God on that final day when we said our final farewell. We moved to St Mary's and that's where I had my first season ticket and a new wave of heroes arrived. Strachan, Beattie, Adkins and Lambert all gave us hope. We dropped down to League One but along came Saint Markus to raise us from the depths and before we knew it we had risen once again. We were back in the Premier League.

No matter how old I got the dream of walking out onto that hallowed turf lived on. It's a dream that at some stage has united us all and as our opportunity to play faded away we all found our new calling. It was time to take our place in the stands.

The terraces welcomed us with open arms, together we support our team, experiencing the highs and lows as we build those lifelong friendships. We still have our part to play and we can still be in the number.

Whether it be at The Dell in years gone by or now at St Mary's, we make up the chorus to cheer on our team. We sing loud and we sing proud. Others try, but no one sings our song like we do because "**Oh When the Saints**" is our battle cry.

We may not be in the Champions League and have League titles to our name, but we are the Saints. We play our way and we are proud of who we are. 1976, the JPT and relegation survival makes up our DNA.

I never got the chance to sign the contract to become a Saint and never got the chance to make my Southampton debut. I have never felt the feeling of walking out in front of the Southampton faithful, nor feel the rush of adrenaline stood in the tunnel as you hear the faithful begin to roar as our friend Justin would proclaim "Please Welcome the Saints!"

But I always wondered what it would be like. So it got me thinking, what is it really like to be a Saint? How does that really feel?

So I picked up the phone to a few former Saints and this is the result. This book tells the stories of our heroes, from the day they signed to making their debut.
We find out what makes our club so special and what it means to them. Which means this is more than just a book, this is a slice of our history.

It has been a real privilege and an honour to write this book. Spending time with our former heroes hearing their stories and recording them to make sure they are never forgotten. I would like to thank all of the players featured for their time and kindness in helping to make this little book of mine a reality. I would also like to thank Mike Thew who has been a tremendous help in getting this off the ground.

Life of a Saint, for me, is also about giving back and proceeds from this book will be going to support the work of the Ex-Southampton Former Professional Players Association and other charities. So thank you for buying this book and helping to support some very worthy causes that make such a huge contribution to our communities.

One thing I will certainly take away from meeting our Saints heroes is that once you have worn the shirt and you know what that feels like, it's a feeling that never leaves you.

It was overwhelming to hear how much the love and support from the fans really means to them all. It may have been a few years ago since some of them hung up their boots, but trust me to still be received with such love and affection really does mean the world to them.

Our club is very special, the fans are incredible and once you have played for us we never forget you, which just goes to prove:

# ONCE YOU'RE A SAINT, YOU'RE ALWAYS A SAINT.

## Because when we "Go Marching In" there really is no other club like ours.

# LIFE OF A SAINT

# LAWRIE McMENEMY
## M.B.E

MANAGER : 1973 - 1985
Games : 604
Win % : 42.2

### SAINTS HONOURS:
1975 - 1976 FA Cup Winner
1977 - 1978 Second Division Runner Up
1978 - 1979 League Cup Finalist
1983 - 1984 First Division Runner Up

Arguably the greatest Manager ever to take the reins of our club, Lawrie McMenemy led the Saints to FA Cup glory in 1976, writing himself and that team into Southampton legend. Joining Saints from Grimsby Town in the summer of 1973, he already had success having won the fourth division title twice. Joining Ted Bates at the helm, his first season didn't play out as he had hoped with relegation to the Second Division, but the board had faith and it was suitably rewarded.

Lawrie was at the helm for twelve years, signing some of the most iconic players to have ever pulled on the red and white. He took us to Wembley on several occasions and who can forget about us being runners up in the First Division in 1984. Now a proud club ambassador, Lawrie is a man who very much helped shape our club to be what it is today.

### JOINING THE SAINTS - GRIMSBY
"I first met Ted Bates at Lilleshall where the managers would get together every summer for a week's training course. It was good for me from a young manager's point of view because you would mix and mingle with big names in the game. People from the FA would

put on coaching sessions and things like that, but the big thing was the meals together and at night having a drink to get to know these fellas, and that's how I first met Ted and we got on very well.

In the summer of 1973 I remember getting a call asking if I would like to go down for an interview at Southampton to join the management team. What I didn't know until a long time after was that two people had recommended me to Ted and the club: Don Revie who was at Leeds United and Alan Brown who was my Manager at Sheffield Wednesday, where I had been a coach.

When I was at Sheffield Wednesday with Alan Brown he used to make us go to games to watch the opposition, especially Leeds who were a big club. Don Revie always made a point of coming into the room we were all in at the end of the game to have a chat and say hello. So when I was at Doncaster as Manager, I contacted him and asked if there was any chance of a game pre-season. He agreed and sent down a strong team and it turned out he had been keeping an eye on me and my progress.

So I took the interview at Southampton and George Reader the Chairman, Sir George Merrick and Charles Chaplin were there. Now Charles was a lovely guy. He wore a monocle and a fresh carnation every day. I remember someone telling me once that they were coming back from a trip abroad and the Chairman said to the team doctor on the flight to sit with Mr Chaplin and to have your tablets ready as he was not well. So the plane took off and Mr Chaplin asked for a glass of water. The doctor got ready thinking **'Here we go'**. When the glass of water arrives it turns out it was just for his carnation!

So we had a meeting and I got offered the job and I took over from day one. Me and Ted got on famously. For instance, I didn't know my way around London and in those days we went to watch games, I would ring Ted and pick him up from Chilworth. He would show me how to get there and how to get into the club and so on. We went all over, we used to go to the midlands and I remember he drove once and we were coming back along the motorway and out of the blue he shouted **"Whoops"**. I was like what's the matter? **"I've missed the turning"**. Next thing he started reversing back up the motorway.

We were very very close and I would always have a cup of tea with him and talk. For me that's what should happen more now. People my age with my experience wouldn't mind sitting with a young manager and letting them bounce ideas off you."

## FIRST SEASON RELEGATION

"It went down to the last game of the season away to Everton. We won our game but other teams had also won and we went down, third bottom, ironically with more points than Saints had stayed up with the previous three or four seasons.

The week after I was running around the pitch at The Dell on my own and all of a sudden out of the corner of my eye I spot the Chairman and Sir George coming down the stairs and I thought **'Aye aye this is it!'**

The Chairman said **'Manager'**, I thought oh no here we go this is me off, **'Sort it out'**, that's all he said and they turned around and walked back up the steps.

They gave me time and let me change things, but that's how the club and football was back then. Nowadays the Manager will get the sack and the players will go but they gave me time.

I remember at Wembley in 1976, at the end of game after all the handshakes at full time, I looked up to the Directors. They were sat up in the Royal Box in the same row as Her Majesty the Queen and I saw that some of them were shedding a tear. That was a nice moment for me to see them so happy, they stood by me and I had repaid them."

## LAWRIE PLANTS THE SEEDS FOR THE SOUTHAMPTON ACADEMY

"I remember saying to Ted one day **'What's the scouting like here? What do we do?'** Ted looked at me like wondering what the hell I was on about. He said **'Oh we get the best lads in Hampshire'**. I said **'Well Ted you should, but what about the rest of the country?'**

Turns out they pretty much didn't have anybody. The club didn't have a set-up and to be honest not many other clubs did either at the time. So I put scouts in Gateshead and Bristol who would go and find the best players in their areas. They would train them on a weekly basis and in the holidays they would bring the best ones down for me and my staff to have a look at in Southampton.

I would then decide who to give a school boy form to at fourteen and once they had signed that, it meant they couldn't go to another club. When they left school I then had to offer the ones who I thought had a chance to go to the next level an apprenticeship and then at eighteen I had to decide if they had made enough progress to be given a professional contract. They would get either one or two years and what was nice is that the board just let me do all that.

Obviously you couldn't sign everyone and when I let people go I would always sit them down and say I would try and help them get another club. I remember we had Chris Wilder and Alan Knill who are now both at Sheffield United. They were both with us at Southampton and I remember when I let Alan go at the end of his contact. He got up went to the door turned round and said '**I'm going to prove you wrong**' I said '**I hope you do.**'

It turns out he did because when he was at Swansea in 1998, I saw he got a call up to play for Wales v Netherlands. So the next day I sent him a telegram saying '**You proved me wrong**'."

## KEEP GOING DRIVER - ROAD TO WEMBLEY

"When we were in the hotel at Wembley for the cup final, I remember our coach driver was more nervous than the players were. It's easy to forget it was also the biggest day of his life too, along with all of the team. Driving into Wembley it was packed and two fellas who had a couple too many swayed onto the road and got clipped by the bus. I had a look round and saw they were ok and said '**DRIVE ON!**' So he carried on and we got to the stadium a little bit later than planned due to the traffic. We drove in and the players got off and walked out on to the pitch, but because we were a little bit late Manchester United were already there.

Tommy Docherty greeted me and said '**Where have you been?**' Now someone had taken a picture of me and Tommy laughing and there was a caption competition of what was being said in the paper. There were lots of good answers but this is what actually happened. I was telling Tommy the story about us hitting two blokes on the way in and explaining they were ok, but the reason we were laughing was because Tommy said '**Who's got their tickets?**'."

## SOUTHAMPTON WELCOMES BACK THE FA CUP WINNERS
"The bus parade when we came back was very special, I have been told it is still the biggest turn out the city have ever had, even more than after the war. The council had worked out the route and it was going to take forty five minutes, but it ended up taking four and a half hours! You couldn't move for people. I remember at one point we went past a working man's club and outside there was a guy with no clothes on. Apparently he had a bet that if Saints won the cup he would take his clothes off. We won and his pals made him do it as the bus went past and in front of all those people. If I remember rightly, the Echo even put a picture in the paper of him but covered him up with a little rosette."

## LAWRIE'S GREATEST ACHIEVEMENT - 1983 / 1984
"As a Manager, people look at clubs especially like ours and say that winning the FA Cup against Manchester United when we were a second division club must the highlight of my career. But as a Manager in the cup you have to win eight or maybe nine games to lift the trophy.

When you finish second in the league after 42 games, it wasn't 38 like now, and you finish just three points behind Liverpool, that to me was the highlight of my career. People often say '**But you had Keegan, Ball and players like that**' but we didn't, they weren't with us then.

When you look through that team we had some great players like Steve Moran, Peter Shilton, Steve Baker, Mark Dennis, Ivan Golac, Eamonn Collins, Danny Wallace, Steve Williams, Ruben Agboola, Dave Puckett, David Armstrong, Nick Holmes, Peter Shilton and Mick Mills. We had a good mix of young players and experienced professionals.

We had had one hell of a season with an FA Cup Semi Final appearance as well. I remember last game of the season we were playing Notts County away and for some reason, probably because we had that cup run, we were playing after the season had finished. Going into the game we knew that we knew going to finish fifth or sixth, but if we won we were going to finish second.

In the dressing room at half time and we were looking like we were going to lose, we came in and I'm on a right warpath. Mick Mills is sat down looking a bit defeated. So I said '**It's alright for you, you have finished second before**' because of course he had been at a very successful Ipswich side.

I said '**I haven't and they haven't, we are going to finish bloody second**'.

We went out won the game 3-1 and finished second after forty two games just three points behind Liverpool and for me as Manager has got to be the highlight."

## LAWRIE THE MASTER OF THE TRANSFER

"Looking back you have to remember we weren't a wealthy club so I couldn't go big in the market, but we did have a lot of big names. At one stage we had six former England captains in the side. When I got them they were at the end of their careers so I could afford them, their legs might have been going but they still had the brain!

So I put together old heads with young legs and the challenge for me was getting the right balance. Not too many of one or the other."

## McMENEMY SIGNS A WORLD CUP WINNER

"Ahh Alan Ball he was a great player, I had read that he was about to leave Arsenal. He had a wonderful career and of course who can forget 1966 but his playing career was coming towards an end. There was another club involved who wanted him but he decided to come down and he signed for us.

He came in and just loved to play. He was as good off the field as he was on it and that's what clubs are missing these days, somebody on the pitch saying come on, helping the younger players out, talking to them and being a leader.

During the week in the dressing room they would all be listening intently as he would be helping them out and giving them advice.

I still drive past where he used to live now and I always say God Bless you Alan."

## LAWRIE PULLS OFF THE SIGNING OF THE CENTURY - KEEGAN BECOMES A SAINT

"There was an article somewhere I read which said Kevin Keegan might be on the move from Hamburg. Now he was linked with Real Madrid and all the big clubs and I thought Liverpool might have put a clause in the deal when they sold him that they had first shout on him when he left.

The secretary at Liverpool at the time was a guy called Peter Robinson, so I rang him up for a general chat. I said '**I see Keegan might be on the move, is he coming back to you?**' And he went '**No**'.

Somehow I managed to get hold of Kevin's number and I'm not too sure how I did it. We hadn't met each other but in those days everyone kind of knew each other. I just rang him up and had a chat, didn't mention transfers or anything initially, I just asked if he could sign something for a fan. We had a couple of calls and on the third one I said, '**This moving thing, you're probably going to Madrid or something but ever thought about coming back the UK?**' He didn't say yes or no, so I could tell he hadn't decided yet. So I said '**You're more than welcome at Southampton**'. I told him it was a nice area and we had players like Bally and Channon at the club.

He was due over to play for England, so I set up a meeting with him in London. I knew a chap who had a place in Kensington so we agreed to meet there, as I didn't want to meet in a hotel where people could see.

At this stage I still hadn't told anyone at the club, so I spoke with Guy Askcombe who was on the Board and asked him to come along. I said to the fella whose house it was, whom was a big Saints fan that I will answer the door as he didn't know who was coming.

A taxi pulled up outside and Kevin had arrived. We had a general chat and then out of the blue he said '**Have you got a contract?**' which caught me unaware but Guy Askcombe picked up his briefcase and pulled out some papers and Kevin signed a blank contract there and then.

So when it came to announcing it, I rang Alan Montgomery who was at The Sun and I said **'Monday, Potters Heron, bring yourself and all your mates'**. Now he wanted to know what for but I said **'I'm not telling you but you don't want to miss it!'** In those days all the football was on a Saturday so the journalists traditionally had Monday off, but not on that day. I arranged all the timings, booked a function room at the hotel, they all arrived and crammed in still unaware of what was about to unfold.

The next challenge was getting Kevin in, because at that point nobody knew what was about to happen. Hamburg flew him over in a private plane to Southampton Airport and his agent picked him up from there. Initially, Kevin's agent didn't know about any of this and I said to Kevin he really should know, but of course not many players had agents in those days so it isn't like it is now.

I had given the players the day off from training but I asked Alan Ball and Mick Channon to be there, the Chairman was present and everyone was wondering what was going on. Then all of a sudden there was a knock on the door. In walked Jean Keegan with a baby in her arms and behind her in walked Kevin Keegan.

There was a gasp in the room and they all stood up and started clapping. I then made the announcement that Kevin Keegan was signing for Southampton.

Alan Ball, bless him, thought he was going to be on This Is Your Life and it was a set up and that's what we were really there for.

Back in those days, of course, all the journalists had to phone the news stories back up to London, there was no email. So a few of them came back to mine, I filled them all in a bit more and let them use my phone. Kevin was a great player for us and a wonderful guy."

### 1980 - 1981 LAWRIE TO MANCHESTER UNITED?

"We were abroad somewhere with the team and I got a call from Vince Wilson. He was a Geordie who worked in Manchester on the Mirror, he rang me and said **'When are you going to Manchester United?'** So I heard it from him first, but when I got home I got a call from someone at United and by that point it was sinking in a bit.

I remember a few years before Sir Matt Busby invited me to go and speak at the club, we were playing away near Manchester on the Saturday so this particular Friday night worked and my wife Anne was also invited to come with me.

Looking around the room the Board was there and I was sat on the top table with all of them. Anne was sat with all of the Board members wives, and looking back on that night they were interviewing me for the job.

I turned it down though, I could have gone but there were a number of reasons why I didn't. Mainly though it was because of my family. Having moved around a lot in my early career, Durham to Sheffield, Doncaster to Grimsby and then to Southampton we were really settled in Southampton. The kids were settled in school and family wise that was a big factor for me.

I often think should I have gone? Managers never turned down Manchester United. I would have liked the challenge but I think on turning it down it gave me more to prove. I was right to turn it down and finishing second above Manchester United in 83-84. It proved that I could do it and hadn't bottled the challenge."

## THE CLUB IS NOTHING WITHOUT THE FANS
"The fans are everything. I learned at all the clubs I managed that clubs are not just judged on the pitch. They are also judged by their importance to the area and the players have to realise that. I would make the Southampton players go to the hospital at Christmas time, which they still do, and I would get them to go to factories to meet the fans. It was something I first learned at Grimsby. I took the players to the fish docks at 8am in the morning and they were walking around meeting all the dockers while they were hard at work.

We went back to the ground and I said **'Don't get changed we are not training'**. I said **'You see those guys we saw today? They have to work every day to earn enough to come and watch you on a Saturday.'** Every now and again I would remind them of that on a match day and would say **'Remember the dockers they are out there now!'**

It so important for me the players know what the club means to the fans. The people who come have to pay a lot of money to support them and that was something I made sure I did at Southampton too."

# MATTHEW LE TISSIER

**1986 - 2002**
**POSITION:** Attacking Midfield
**APPS:** 462
**GOALS:** 209

**DEBUT:** 30/09/1986 v Norwich City

**SAINTS HONOURS:** PFA Young Player of the Year 1989 - 1990, 1992 Zenith Data Cup Runner Up, 1989 - 1990 / 1993 - 1994 & 1994 - 1995 Player of the Year, 1994 - 1995 Premier League PFA Team of the Year, 1994 - 95 English Football Goal of the Season

The man, the legend and the icon that is Matthew Le Tissier is a player who is synonymous with our great club. If you ask fans from other clubs to name a Southampton legend I would say nine times out of ten they would say Le Tissier. Born and raised in Guernsey, Matt crossed the English Channel to join the Saints and signed YTS forms in 1985 before signing his first professional contact in 1986.

In a career lasting seventeen years we saw moments of magic season after season as Le Tissier weaved his magic on the field. With record scoring penalty ability he was a player Southampton relied upon season after season and who knows if Saints would have survived those relegation battles without him. The honour of scoring the final ever league goal at The Dell v Arsenal in 2001 could go to only one man and that was him. The first midfielder to score one hundred Premier League goals, Matt won three player of the year titles, a PFA Young Player of the Year Award, but there can never be enough recognition for the man we call **"LE GOD"**.

## GUERNSEY BOY TAKES FLIGHT

"I was spotted playing in a game for Guernsey at Millbrook playing fields. I was playing on the right wing that day instead of my usual position of centre midfield which was where I played growing up. The club invited me for a week's trial so I made my way across from Guernsey. They played me out on the right wing in the trial because that is where they had seen me playing, not my usual central midfield role. I didn't say anything though because I was just so happy to be there to be honest.

After that one week of training they said they wanted to sign me as an associate school boy and I was like '**Wow**' all this after just one week!

In the school holidays I would head back to Southampton for more training and when I was at the end of my fifth year at school the decision was going to be made on whether I was going to be an apprentice or not.

I remember the news came via a letter in the post, my parents had opened it and when I got back from school they said '**Read that**' and again I was like '**Oh Wow!**'

This all happened mid May and Saints were offering me a place on their youth training scheme starting on the 1st July. '**6 weeks and I'm there!**' I was so excited but I also knew my whole life was about to change completely and be turned upside down in six weeks.

I was going to be living in a house with people I didn't know and I would have no family around me at the age of sixteen. This was a big deal, so I was feeling a whole mixture of emotions from being excited and chuffed but also a bit scared."

## SOUTHAMPTON CALLS

"The first person I met from the club on that first day was John Mortimer. I had no idea where I was and no idea where I was going to be sleeping that night.

Sir John picked me up in his car and said '**We're going to drive you to where you're going to be staying for the next two years.**' I turned up at the house in Lordshill, knocked on the door and this big bloke opened it and went '**Alright nipper!**'

I'll never forget that first day. I got introduced to my hosts, took my bags up to my bedroom and then I got taken straight to The Dell to do a bit of training.

That night I came back to my digs for dinner. Pat, the lady who I was staying with, had done a nice looking salad for my evening meal. Now, I'd never had a salad in my life and I looked at the plate and went **'Oh what's that?'** to which Pat said **'Don't you like salad?'** and I went **'I've never had one'**. To which she replied **'Oh okay would you like some sausage and chips?'** and I was like **'Yes please!'**

That was my introduction to Southampton and my introduction to digs. I was there for three and a bit years I think in the end. The club paid for my accommodation while I was an apprentice and after I turned professional it was then up to me to pay my way. So I paid to stay there a little bit longer until I got my first flat in Portswood."

## LE TISSIER TURNS PRO

"There were no guarantees of getting a professional contract, but I kind of knew I was going to be offered one because I made my debut before my eighteenth birthday, and that was how the decision was made whether or not you were going to be a pro.

So I had a fairly good idea that I was going to be taken on. I remember going up to Chris Nicholls office and all the other lads that had been in before me were given one year contracts. So I was kind of expecting the same, but when he put the piece of paper in front of me and told me he was going to give me a contract, I was expecting to see one year written down but he was offering me two years! It was £100 a week in the first year and I got a rise in the second to £120 a week. I was chuffed to bits to have been offered my first professional contract and couldn't have been happier."

## THE FIRST TEAM DEBUT

"My debut was away at Norwich. I had played a couple of times pre-season, we went down to Torquay and Exeter and we also had a game v Benfica at The Dell for Nick Holmes testimonial which I also played in. I wasn't in the squad for the first couple of games of the season and next up was away to Norwich. I think there had been an injury and Chris Nicholl called me up to the squad. There was only one sub in those days and only thirteen of us travelled so I had a 50/50 chance of being on the bench.

When the squad was announced I was on the bench. I had a real chance of making my debut. We were losing 3-2 and then I got the call to go on with fifteen minutes from the end. I would like to say I made the difference and we won, but we ended up losing 4-3.

Regardless of the result, to have made my debut in the First Division was pretty special. Having grown up with the goal to play in the First Division and play for England, I was on my way and the journey had begun.

My first team debut at The Dell followed on the Tuesday night. Chris Nicholl called me to his office on the Monday morning after the game at Norwich, and looking back this was brilliant for him to do as I don't think all Managers would do that. He knew my family was back in Guernsey and they would probably want to see my full debut. So he called me in and said **'You're going to be playing tomorrow night. I'm starting you so if you want to phone your family that should be enough time to get flights to come over and watch.'**

I think there were about twenty three members of the family that actually came across for the game. It was a mad rush for them all to get over as there weren't many seats left on the plane and I think a couple of them even got on a boat to make it.

My mum and dad tell a story that they couldn't travel together because there was only one seat left on the plane. So mum said to dad **'You take that seat. I will find my way'**, and I think she was one of the ones who got a boat to that game.

We won the game 2-0 under the lights at The Dell; growing up I was a Spurs fan so playing against Glenn Hoddle who was my hero in my home debut added to the occasion and made it a very special night.

It was all a pretty awesome experience, I did alright in the match and I thought at that point that I could make a career out of this."

## THE FIRST HAT-TRICK v LEICESTER

"Later on that season in the March, we were playing Leicester City at The Dell, it was snowing and I remember it was absolutely freezing. My dad came over sporadically for games as my parents couldn't afford to come every week to watch me play as the flights weren't cheap, but luckily this was one of the games that dad came to watch.

We won 4-0 and I scored my first hat-trick. To have my dad in the stands that day was incredibly special. At full time I was given the match ball and I got the whole team to sign it. I gave it to my mum and dad and it was one of the coolest moments of my life to give them the match ball after all the support they had given me."

## LE TISSIER'S STAND OUT GOALS

"I would say there are probably three goals that stand out above all the others. The first would be my goal against Newcastle where I flicked the ball over a couple of defenders before putting it in the bottom corner. That one was a big moment in my career. Ian Branfoot had dropped me for the previous five games and I came back into the team. It was live on Sky and I scored two really good goals in the game. Those goals catapulted me back into the fray, as at that point my career was just starting to go the wrong way a little bit. So that was a massive turning point. After that game I went from strength to strength and the confidence that gave me was amazing. I ended up being the Captain of the team six weeks later after scoring 25 goals, so that was a pretty big moment for me...and that's why that goal is a special one to me.

Another one I scored against Blackburn at Ewood Park I would say was my favourite ever goal. Thirty five yards out and it was a shot I had been practicing a lot in training. Throw in the fact that it was against an old team mate of mine Tim Flowers, who said I'd never score against him when he left Saints, made it pretty special.

And then the last goal at The Dell, which just capped it all off really. It was a dream ending to that day. If you had written it as a script people would have said **'You can't write that, that's too farfetched!'** I hadn't scored a Premier League goal all season. I had been injured most of it and to come off the bench and score a goal like that in the last couple of minutes was pretty amazing. Of course throw in the fact that it was a winning goal. which moved the club up the table. I think it was two or three places we jumped because it earned the club another couple of million pounds in prize money. That was my last ever goal for Southampton so not a bad a way to finish."

## SOUTHAMPTON v ARSENAL A GOODBYE TO THE DELL

"Having been injured most of that season I had only just got back training with the lads and Stuart Gray was absolutely brilliant with me and Franny. We weren't in any danger of relegation so it was a lovely opportunity for him to be able to say to me and Franny '**For what you two have done for the club over these last fifteen years, you deserve to be on the pitch for that last game. So whatever happens on Saturday, you and Franny will be on the pitch at the end of the game**' and that was really a nice touch. He told us that on the Tuesday before the game and I remember every night going to bed for the rest of that week just thinking how I was going to score the last goal at The Dell.

If I'm honest I didn't dream about anything that spectacular. Whenever I visualised the goal in my dreams it was always with my right foot because that was the one I was a little bit better with, but I was always confident if a chance fell in the box it didn't really matter which foot it was on. I had practiced enough with my left foot that if something was on I was more than capable of producing a finish. So it wasn't the way I was dreaming about scoring it...but I will take it."

## THE DELL, THE HOME OF LE GOD

"It was an amazing place for me. Ninety nine percent of my career was played at The Dell as I only played a couple of times at St Mary's, so for me The Dell was my home.
It was my stage, it's where I felt the most comfortable and it was just an amazing quirky little football ground which a lot of players from opposition did not like coming to play at. That was a nice feeling to have when your home ground was so homely that people didn't really want to come into your house.

The Dell was definitely one of the reasons I think we stayed up so many years when we were struggling. The crowd really got behind you when the chips were down, it was a pretty special atmosphere."

## BE IN THAT NUMBER...7

"The number 7, it kind of just happened really that for the first six years of my career I wore all sorts of numbers. I had worn the eight, eleven and nine. I don't think I ever wore the number ten, which is quite odd considering I would have been the main candidate for that role.

When the Premier League came in they said everyone was to have a squad number and for that season I was given the number 7. It could've been anything really, so it was just luck of the draw on the day, but it's a pretty good number that's been associated with great players down the years at Saints".

## XAVI "LE TISSISER MY IDOL"

"That was pretty good to hear, I mean he was a pretty decent footballer himself who had done everything in the game. For him to actually come out in public and say that he enjoyed watching me play as a kid growing up I was like '**That's nice**'.

I had a lovely moment last year when I played in the BMW Pro Am at Wentworth. I was drawn in a group with Pep Guardiola. On the day I was on the putting green before we were due to go out, Pep still hadn't shown up yet and there was only about ten minutes before we were due to tee off.

All of a sudden he walks onto the putting green. So I thought I'd better go introduce myself. I shook his hand and said, **'I'm Matt Le Tissier, I'm playing golf with you today'** and he turned around to me and said, **'You don't have to introduce yourself to me. I remember you scoring all these goals from thirty five yards'**.

So I was like **'Nice, Pep Guardiola has even heard of me'** and I thought did anyone else hear that? If I tell this to people they're not going to believe me! I turned round and Flash (Gordon Watson), who was caddying for the day, just looked at me and said **'Yep I heard it!'**."

## PFA YOUNG PLAYER OF THE YEAR AWARD

"The PFA awards are awards that get voted for by the players around you and the players you played against which made it extra special. So to win was a real honour. People often forget that it was a pretty good year for Saints because Rodney Wallace was also in the top three. It would've been a proud day for Dave Merrington to have two of his lads that he brought through to finish first and third in the PFA awards. Five years later he had the same again when Alan Shearer won the PFA Player of the Year award and I came runner up.

For me, accolades are nice but I always like to think how it feels for someone else, especially someone like Dave who put so much effort and so much commitment into his job. He was amazing at what he did for us boys back then and is a man who had a massive influence on my career."

## ALAN BALL

"The moment he walked into The Dell was the moment my career really took off. Those eighteen months he was my manager were the best eighteen months of my career.

He had a belief in me which no other manager really did. They all kind of paid lip service to the fact that I had some ability and the crowd liked me. I got the feeling that some managers felt like they had to play me because of the crowd.

But not Alan Ball. He played me because he truly believed that I was a really good footballer and that took me to a different level. He was an amazing man, how he would make you feel going out on a football pitch was just brilliant.

Away from the touch line and on the training pitch he was also brilliant. He had his ups and downs; he had his mood swings like all managers and he had players that frustrated him. Luckily I was on the right side of him, but there were players who will have a very different opinion of him because of the way that he was with them. If he didn't feel you were a good enough player he could be a little bit dismissive of you, so I could understand why some players didn't like him as much as did.

I could sit and listen to him for hours and when we used to have dinner together, I remember at the end of evening's just walking away thinking that I had hardly said a word and I absolutely loved it. He was so passionate about everything he loved in life.
If anybody asks me who my favourite Manager was it would be Alan Ball."

## TED BATES

"When I was at the club obviously Ted wasn't as involved as much as he had been in the past. But I can still remember as a young player I would be at The Dell during the week and would see Ted even at the ripe old age he was then still doing laps of The Dell in his kit. It was amazing that he still wanted to be part of it, having a little jog around the ground to keep himself in the best shape he possibly could.

He always came to away games and would be sat at the front of the bus. He was there if you wanted to chat with him but he wouldn't push himself on you. He was really chilled and you knew where he was if you wanted to have a chat. I thought it was a lovely way to do things and I have of a lot respect for what Ted did for the Football Club. He was an amazing servant and has rightly got that statue right outside the front of the stadium."

## TEAMMATES

"When I first got into the team Jimmy Case was brilliant for me. He was an experienced old head that taught me so much, he looked after the youngsters in the team. He was the minder in midfield and he made sure that we weren't getting bullied by the opposition. I loved playing alongside Rodney Wallace. Rodney was very much underrated and in the two seasons we played together we almost got 100 goals between us. His pace was electric, he could finish with both feet across the ball well and was really brave in possession.

Moving on a little bit I enjoyed playing with Ronnie Ekelund; he had a brilliant footballing brain and we were on the same wavelength from the second he turned up to training.

There were also lots of players who stood up to be counted when relegation seemed a real possibility. You had players like Francis Benali and he would be my first pick if I needed to select a team to stay up on the last day of the season.

I played with some unbelievable centre backs; Dean Richards, God bless him, was a fantastic defender and Russell Osman was one of the best two footed footballers I have ever played with.

There are just so many players that I've enjoyed playing alongside down the years. I think more than individuals I most of all just enjoyed playing in a team. Team sports are very underrated as a life skill. You have to learn so many things, for example to get on with people whom if you weren't the same football team then you probably wouldn't spend a minute of your life with. But come Saturday at three o'clock, you would be willing to put your body on the line for them. That's such a good life skill to have. Being able to compartmentalise things so you just keep your focus without getting distracted by personal situations or people that you perhaps don't particularly like, but you have to get on with because they're in the same team."

## MATT LE TISSIER DID LIKE TRAINING!

"Believe it or not Matt Le Tissier did love training! As long as there was a football involved! What I didn't like was the first two or three weeks of pre-season training where we didn't see a football and all we did was just run and do circuit training. It was all the stuff that you had to do to be fit enough to go out and play on a Saturday come the first day of the season, but I didn't like it. It never came natural to me and it was hard for me. I wasn't a naturally fit person but I knew I had to do it to be able to play the game that I loved. So for about three weeks of the year I hated being a footballer and the rest of it was magnificent."

## PROLIFIC FROM THE SPOT

"I don't remember taking too many penalties as a kid. I remember missing one in a big game for the Guernsey under fifteen's against Jersey which was the biggest game of the year. I had a penalty to win the game just before the end of the match and I missed the target. I was devastated and I remember looking back on it and I was just overthinking it too much.

I could remember just staring into one corner to try and make the goalkeeper think I'm going that way. I was just staring and I didn't look at the corner I was gonna put it in because I was so intent on making the goalkeeper think I was going the other way. I took the penalty and put it wide by about a foot. So after that I thought maybe I shouldn't think about it quite so much!

I then started taking penalties for the Southampton Youth Team and in fact I missed one in my first game for them against Reading. I took it well and it was on target but the keeper made a good save. I think the worst thing you could do with a penalty was not hit the target, for me you have to make the goalkeeper make the save.

I didn't let the miss affect me and I carried on taking them for the youth team. I didn't miss another one for ages. When I was twenty one and in the first team we had a competition in training to pick a penalty taker. A couple of the players had missed two or three penalties and Chris Nicholl said **'Whoever wins this competition is going to be the penalty taker for the rest the season'** and I was like **'Yeah I fancy this'**. So I really concentrated and I didn't miss a single one so Chris made me the penalty taker and that was it.

The first season I was penalty taker we got eight penalties. Which was quite a good number and that boosts your tally so I ended up with twenty four goals that season. The following season we got seven and I scored twenty three goals.

As a forward it's an easy way to boost your goal tally. I say easy, but there is pressure on it and you're putting yourself in a position to be shot at, but I enjoyed that. I looked forward to taking penalties and I liked it when I knew everybody in the stadium was looking at me. Everyone in the stadium is watching this standoff between the keeper and the striker and that kind of appealed to my ego."

### LE GOD HANGS UP HIS BOOTS

"It wasn't a nice time, I made the decision while playing in a reserve game at St Mary's. I had had a load of calf strains that season; it got to February or March and I was playing for the reserves to build my fitness back up. Twenty five minutes in and my calf went again. I walked off the pitch, down the tunnel and made my way into the medical room. My testimonial was coming up at the end of the season and my contract was due to expire at that time too. I got to the medical room, sat on the bench and thought, '**I just can't do this anymore**'.

My body was telling me I couldn't do it anymore and I decided there and then that at the end of the season that's it, my testimonial would be the last year of my career and I'm not ashamed to say I sat there and bawled my eye's out."

## ST MARY'S SAY THANK YOU - LE TISSIER'S TESTIMONIAL
"It was quite some turnout, I was really chuffed. I rang up a load of the players I played against, all Ex-England internationals, and the response from them was brilliant.

They all wanted to come down and play, it was absolutely fantastic. Gazza, Chris Waddle, John Barnes...all these magnificent players that when I picked up the phone said '**I'll be there**'. I had a lovely turnout from the fans too.

The game was great fun which is what I wanted it to be, I didn't want it to be serious. My brothers were good footballers and two of them lost a load of weight so they could play and my other brother was a ref so he refereed the game.

It was a lovely family occasion and my committee at the end of the game had organised for a loads of my goals to be played on the big screen with Frank Sinatra's 'My Way' playing. It was a really nice way to finish off my career."

## ALWAYS OUR LE TISSIER
"For me, the love and support I receive from the fans is the justification to me for all those decisions I made to stay at Southampton my whole career when offers came my way to leave.

I love making time for the fans. I remember seeing players when I was a kid waiting for autographs and seeing players that didn't bother and it was just so disappointing. I remember thinking if I ever get in that position I'm never going to turn down giving anyone an autograph. I will take the time and if it means I'm late for something then so be it. The fans are good enough to want to come and queue up and get a signature from you or a photograph so why shouldn't I take the time to do that for them, it doesn't cost anything.

The fans were always a big reason why I stayed at Southampton. The way they treated me right from when I was a kid at seventeen sat on the bench and them singing my name to come. They always made me feel like I was really special to them and I wanted to reciprocate that. I've always said that they were a huge part of the reason why I stayed my whole career."

LIFE OF A SAINT

# JIMMY CASE

1985 - 1991
**POSITION** : Midfield
**APPS** : 269
**GOALS** : 14

**DEBUT:** 23/03/1985 v Tottenham

**SAINTS HONOURS :** 1988 -1989
Player of the Year

Jimmy Case signed for Southampton in the March of 1985 from Brighton and Hove Albion. Lawrie McMenemy's last signing would prove to be yet another player who would win their place in the heart of Saints fans. The no-nonsense midfielder brought a wealth of experience to the side having previously won four first division titles and three European Cups during his time at Liverpool.

Jimmy would go on to captain the Saints and was instrumental in helping bring through a generation of talent that included: Alan Shearer, Matt Le Tissier, Jason Dodd and the Wallace brothers. Never one to shy away from a challenge, Jimmy formed a formidable partnership in midfield with Glenn Cockerill which made Southampton a side no one looked forward to playing against especially at the Dell.

### A EUROPEAN CUP WINNER BECOMES A SAINT

"I was with Brighton at the time and the Manager, Chris Cattlin, said Lawrie McMenemy had been on the phone trying to get me down to Southampton. Brighton were in the Second Division and I was three years into a five year contract. We had been relegated and I was one of those players who wanted to help them get back up rather than just jump ship. The team had been broken up; Guy Stevens went to Tottenham, Steve Foster went off to Aston Villa, Michael Robinson went to the Liverpool and the team was torn apart really. I got call in the February with just ten games left to go until the end of the season. Lawrie wanted someone to go in to the dressing room that would not be overawed by the people in there. The club had players like Peter Shilton, Mick Mills and Joe Jordan at the time and I was the player he wanted. I found out later that Chris Cattlin had gone to the board at Brighton and said **'We should sell Jimmy because I think his legs have gone.'**

I was sold and made the move to Southampton for £30,000; I ended up playing at the club for seven seasons so that made a real mockery of what Chris said about my legs!

I met Lawrie at the club, we sat down and it didn't take me long to sign a contract. I don't know how we got through the medical because I had a groin strain at the time, but there wasn't really much of a medical in them days anyway. There was no running involved or anything like that, the doctors came in and gave you a few X-rays and that was it.

I played my first game away at Tottenham and played in all the games until the end of the season and then Lawrie went to Sunderland."

## THE SAINTS DRESSING ROOM IN 1985

"There were some big characters in that dressing room, the likes of Peter Shilton and especially Joe Jordan, but once it in there and you spend time outside of training with them they are totally different. Joe was one of the most mildly mannered people in the world, but on the pitch he was formidable.

Initially I used to travel backwards and forwards from Brighton, I would come down for training and then go back afterwards, but after a few weeks Joe would invite me over for lunch with his family. They were a great bunch of lads who really looked out for you.

Players like Mick Mills, Nick Holmes and Charlie George were just really nice people, I fitted in easily really."

## CAPTAIN CASE

"That next season Chris Nicholl was appointed Manager and was asked to put his mark on the side. I was given the Captain's armband and he started bringing in the younger players to the side. Maybe he felt I was useful to the team and would be helpful with the kids. I always tried to help the kids in training and made sure they were alright. So I think that Chris saw that quality in me and with my experience he felt I was the perfect candidate."

## ONE YEAR AT A TIME

"I was on a one year contract when I signed for Lawrie. It was for ten games and then the next season. I was thirty one and was told I was signed as a stopgap. Usually in those days players played till about thirty three and then ran a pub, but I went beyond that. I couldn't tell you why because I can't say I looked after myself!

Every year I had to go to Chris Nicholl and sort out my new contract. When it got to the end of the season I would go into his office with the programme from the last game. I would go to the appearances page and run my finger down it and point out my appearances for the season. My name would pretty much be in every week and I would say **'I played all those...I missed those two games because I was booked too many times and being a ball winning midfield player I'm going to get a yellow card every now and again...I missed that one cause I had a knock. So if that doesn't warrant a new contract, I don't know what does'**.

Chris would have square pieces of paper and he would write something on it then slide it across the desk and that would be the offer. He would slide another which was maybe a bonus or something like that. I would normally see him on a Friday, so I would push it back and say **'Put it this way Chris, I will come in Monday and sign for that but I know you can go to the Directors and get me a bit more. So I will leave it with you, but I will still sign for that on Monday'**. Went in on the Monday and he always got me a bit more."

## TAKING ON LIVERPOOL

"We beat Liverpool a few times during my career at Southampton, even at Brighton I beat them once or twice. I remember I scored against them when we played at Anfield in 1990. We lost 3-2 but I put us ahead just after halftime. We went on to lose 3-2 with Ian Rush getting a late winner. For some reason I always had success against them, I know Ronnie Whelan was frightened of me and didn't want to come near me as he always tells now. For me I didn't necessarily want to get one over on them or anything, but a lot of players leave Liverpool and don't do anything, whereas I just went on and on.

At Southampton Chris Nicholl had put together a good side with some great youngsters, with Shearer, Matt Le Tissier and the Wallace brothers. Throw in the midfield players I had around me and it worked well and that brought the success that it did.

I remember when we won 4-1 at The Dell, it just went to show the calibre of the players we had with Matt Le Tissier and Rodney Wallace who got two that day. There was myself and Glenn Cockerill in the midfield and defensively we were strong with Russell Osman and Neil Ruddock at the back. It wasn't a bad Liverpool team we faced on that day and they had some quality but they didn't like the closeness of The Dell. I remember coming there with other clubs and it was always a difficult place to come. We played well that day and got the result. I probably sunk a few pints after that one!"

## BRINGING THROUGH THE NEXT GENERATION
"All of the young players who came through had tremendous ability. I spent a lot of time with them training everyday and I would always push them to make them better. I used to, for example, kick lumps out of Matt Le Tissier because it got him going…I would give him the ball all the time to make him play. He loved beating people and scoring goals. If he had a defender on him in training I would still give him the ball because he then had to do something with it and learn to get out of that situation. He was player who always needed a challenge so I tried to give it to him.

Alan Shearer was always working hard at his game. Myself and Dennis Rofe would stay back afterwards and we would just feed balls. He would spend hours lashing them in the net, no goalkeeper, just working hard on technique and finishing. I played in both of their debuts and who can forget Shearer when he got three v Arsenal in his first game?

The club had some good players coming through when I was there, players like Francis Benali, Jason Dodd and Tim Flowers. In games, I would look out for them and help them though, talking to them saying **'Why don't you come in here a bit'** or **'Look for that ball next time'**."

## PRE-MATCH PASTA

"Chris Nicholl introduced us to nutrition and on a match day we used to go for a pre-match pasta. We would go down at Margaritas which was by the Mayflower and we would eat and then go straight to the game.

Kicking off at three o'clock for me it would sit in your stomach, so I didn't like the pasta. Don't get me wrong, I like pasta ordinarily but not before a game! I said this to the Manager and he tried to explain that it would give me the energy I needed for the game. Now I got that but I said to him **'If I eat that I'm going to be sick on the pitch'**. Throughout my career all I used to have was fillet steak with some toast and a cup of tea before a game.

At Liverpool you used to get a choice: battered fish, chicken or fillet steak with toast and tea and I always went for steak. So that was something I then ate before every game. At Southampton they then told me how it takes eighteen hours to digest and that takes blood from all over my body which should be going to my legs for the game.

Now, I had been eating this steak for ten years and I had never had a problem, won all those trophies and it had never been an issue. They kept trying to make me have pasta and I understood it but it didn't work for me. In the end I won and I kept having my steak, toast and tea."

## TEAM BONDING

"After games you used to go into the players' lounge and have a few drinks and then we would end up in Bedford Place. Not everyone came, but players like Glenn Cockerill, Jerry Forest and whoever wanted to did come, but we never used to drink after Wednesday in the week or before the game, no-one really did. We might drink all Sunday but not before a game.

The Christmas party was always good fun and I was in charge of organising that. We used to fine the lads for certain things throughout the season, if they were late for example or wore a bad tie to a match. All the money got collected and went towards the party.

You would have to ask the Manager when you could organise it for because they had to give it the okay. On the day of the party they would get you in for training in the morning, run you like mad and then give you the day off the next day to recover. One year I went in to see Chris Nicholl and he said '**How much have you got for the party? Because I will match it**' I only had about £480 but straight away I said '**£980**' and without hesitation he gave me another £980 to go out with, so we did alright that year!

I always organised a full Christmas dinner for the team and we had the youngsters along too. We would go to the Dog and Duck by the Old Round house in Southampton as I knew the manager and he had a function room we could use.

We did it in two sittings, I got all the youngsters in first and all the first team had to serve them. I remember one of them started clicking his fingers saying '**My man, my man**' to Peter Shilton '**Could I have a half a lager please?**' which was very funny. We would then swap over and then the day would go on. I always had taxis organised to get everyone home and they were always great nights.

Getting everybody together was a big thing especially with the youngsters because you never knew when you were going to need them and they were going to step up to the first team."

### THE ONE THAT GOT AWAY
"When I first joined the club you obviously didn't know who was who and it took time to get to know everyone. I remember I came into training one week and I found out that that Dave Merrington was at the club and running the youth team.

Going back when I was seventeen I went to Burnley for a trail. I went in for three days with a friend of mine and we were both playing for South Liverpool in the Non-League.

At the end of the three days I got called in to see their youth development officer, who at the time was Dave Merrington and he said '**We don't think you will ever make it in to the professional game, sorry lad.**' I was devastated thinking that was my chance gone.

Fast forward a few years and I had a pretty successful career, won a few trophies and I was now at Southampton. So I caught up with Dave and we had a chat and laughed about it, but from that point on every morning I would say to Dave '**I'm the one that got away hey?**' It was always a bit of fun but it was funny how it all panned out, I always say when I am speaking to anyone with kids who want to make it in the game that all of us who made it had bumps along the way like I did."

## THE FANS

"The crowd was always on your side and I felt that I was well liked. Mainly because of the way I played and my attitude towards the club. I would get on with the game, I had a little bit of aggression and made sure everyone was pulling their weight.

Having that relationship with the fans was what it was all about, when you play for a club it's all about them, without them there is no club. For us midfielders it's a different relationship compared to a striker who goes out and gets all the goals. We are the engine room and sometimes it's unsung but it's essential and the fans support on a match day meant so much.

To still be recognised by the fans means a lot. Looking back it means you obviously did something right and you gave them something to cheer about. I had a real rapport with them and even now when we do events. The fans love to have chat and I had a great time at the club and the fans were, and still are, really great."

# LIFE OF A SAINT

# JOHN SYDENHAM

**1956 - 1970**
**POSITION** : Winger
**APPS** : 401
**GOALS** : 40

**DEBUT:** 04/05/1957 v Newport County

**SAINTS HONOURS** : 1965 - 1966 Second Division Runner Up

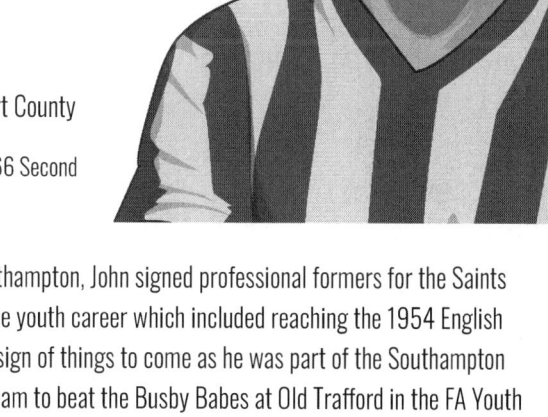

Born in 1939 and raised in Southampton, John signed professional formers for the Saints in 1957 having had a remarkable youth career which included reaching the 1954 English School trophy. This would be a sign of things to come as he was part of the Southampton youth side who were the first team to beat the Busby Babes at Old Trafford in the FA Youth Cup winning 3-2.

Sydenham would go on to forge a remarkable partnership with Terry Paine, arguably the finest pair of wingers the club has ever seen. The pair became a trio in the 1965 - 1966 season when Sydenham, Paine and Martin Chivers set the Second Division on fire and secured Saints promotion to the First Division for the very first time when they helped Saints to secure the runners up spot.

### GROWING UP A SAINT
"I went to my first Saints game when I was eight, so over seventy two years ago and from there I started following Saints and never missed a game.

My playing career began playing with the Southampton Schoolboys; I was fortunate enough to be in a team that got into the National Schools Final. We played at Anfield against the Liverpool Schoolboys, I would have been fourteen and it really all started from there. We used to go and train in The Dell and we used to meet some of the players there that were my heroes. When I left school I managed to break into the youth team and we had brilliant team. I was fortunate to be in teams that were doing well and that meant you were being seen by people from the club. As schoolboys we also played our home games at The Dell with incredible form. Our shirts were laid out and I can even remember the smell of the shirts to this very day. Even at that age it meant so much to me to be playing for Southampton."

### THE YOUNG SAINTS BEAT THE BUSBY BABES

"Playing against Matt Busby and the United team was very special. We lost at The Dell but when we went to Old Trafford we beat them 3-2. We were the first team to beat them there and Matt Busby came into the dressing room to congratulate us. He was the number one Manager in the country at the time so it was all very exciting."

### BECOMING A PROFESSIONAL SAINT

"You didn't have apprenticeships when I was growing up so when I was seventeen I signed a professional contract. Terry Paine was six months older than me so he'd signed just before me and he got in the team straightaway. My first game came at the end of that season and I played in the game v Newport County at The Dell which was just amazing. I just couldn't believe what I was doing. That was my first game and then the following season I started playing more regularly.

I remember when I signed for the club I got a £10.00 signing on fee and I rode my bike over to The Dell to pick it up. I rode all the way home up Lancers Hill waving this cheque to all my mates shouting **'I've just signed for the Saints!'** I was so excited and proud.

It was such a great time to be a Saint; Ted Bates's attitude to everything was to just basically go and attack everybody. As long as we got more goals than the opposition that was his motto. For me, as being an out and out winger, he would say **'Just take him on, take him on'**. That was always what I could hear from the bench. I was one on one with the fullback and I would hear Ted shouting **'Take him on'** and that was what you were encouraged to do. Nobody worried about whether you were going to get back afterwards, you got back when you could. That was my main role and it was the same for Terry on the other side of the pitch. I played regularly for the team until it came to National Service when I was twenty which then meant I had two years away."

## SYDENHAM'S DEBUT v NOTTS COUNTY
"Ted would always call you into the office to tell you that you were making your debut. I got the call to go in and speak with him ahead of the last game of the season. There were only about ten thousand fans there but to me it could have been fifty thousand. Making my first team debut at The Dell was just a dream come true.

For me to be in the first team playing alongside players that were my absolute heroes was incredible and here I was out on the field alongside them, it was amazing.

Having played at The Dell quite a few times before in schoolboys and youth teams, I knew the feeling of running down those steps and out on to the pitch, but this time it was different. This time it was for the first team and this was just unbelievable for me. There was a guy called Johnny Walker who was inside left to me at the time and he really helped me through the game right from the kick off. He encouraged me, he was alongside me all the time, he gave me a lot of confidence and you just never forget that kind of support."

## TED BATES
"I always got on really well with Ted. Not everybody did obviously, there were players that came and left and players that fell out with him in different ways, but I think for both myself and Terry Paine we had a great relationship with him right from the start. Even when I got called for National Service and went into the army for two years he stood by me. He has said to me **'Don't worry as soon as you're back, you get back in the team'**.

I missed a couple of vital years at that time but I'll never forget the way he stood by me. He believed in me 100% and when you have the backing from the Manager it's great for you as a player. I had a great relationship with Ted, he was the only Manager I played for at the club and I was the only player to have played 400 games all under him."

## NATIONAL SERVICE FOR A SAINT

"National Service was something I really didn't want to do, I didn't like the thought that was going to be away from the Saints for two years. At that time National Service was coming to an end so it just seemed to me to be a waste of time.

In hindsight now looking back on everything I had a wonderful time in those two years with the army. I did play some games for Southampton occasionally but while away I got to play for the British Army team and we toured the world. The problem I had though was because I was good at football they made me play for all the teams. You had the Army HQ team, D Company side and Medical Corps team to name but a few. I used to wake up and think **'Where am I and where am I playing today?'**

I always remember Southampton were playing Liverpool in an evening game at The Dell and the Army said that they would let me go to play in that game, but I had to play five days in a row before that for all these different teams. As long as I did that they would let me play for the Saints.

So I played in all the games and they let me come home for the Liverpool game. I remember they sent a taxi up to the camp for me and I got to The Dell an hour before kickoff. I got changed for the game in the dressing room with all the lads and out we went. We won the game 4-1 and at full time all the lads were off for a few beers, but not me. The taxi was outside waiting and I had to go straight back to base.

It was really tough at times but I played with some wonderful players in the Army. There were a lot of great players that got called for National Service that I travelled the world with. Players like Ron Yates, Jim Baxter, Alec Young and Johnny Byrne. It was a fantastic team to play in, but of course it's two years out of your life and two years out of what is a very short career."

## MEMORABLE MOMENTS

"There are quite a few games that stick out. 1963 which was the year of the big freeze in England is one of those moments. All football was off and we flew to Jersey just to train as it was frozen everywhere.

That was a fantastic year because we ended up getting in to the FA Cup Semi-Final, but the thing was because games were being played so quickly after the big freeze you lost track of where you were. You were playing cup games one weekend then replays on the Wednesday, then next round and before we knew where we were, we were in the Semi-Final.

We beat Nottingham Forest in the Quarter-Final. I remember we were 3-0 down at The Dell with ten minutes to go and we clawed it back to 3-3 before winning the replay 5-0 at their place.

The Semi-Final was probably one of the most disappointing days of my life in football. We lost 1-0 to Manchester United. Denis Law scored a scrappy goal and we just never played our game and they didn't either, it was a miserable game and unfortunately the result didn't go our way.

We had a little group of players that organised some fundraising at that time for us and if we had gone into the final it would have been worth £10,000 to each us. You can only imagine what would have meant to us financially in 1963.

4-1 win v Manchester United in 1969 also stands out. It was at Old Trafford and was one of my last games for Southampton. United had started the season really badly. I think they had lost their first two or three games and things were going really badly. By this time Ted had changed our style of play a lot because when we were playing those sort of teams with players like Best, Law, Charlton we became very defensively minded. That day was an amazing day though, Ron Davies scored all four goals and I had a good day setting up a few. After that match, sadly, I only played a few handfuls of games.

There was also a 9-3 against Wolves. I think we were 3-1 down at one stage, we got back into the game and at the end it could have been 15-3 to us.

In 1960 we beat Man City in the Cup 5-1 at their place. We were in the Third Division at the time and they were in the First Division. It never got a lot of publicity but it was an amazing result. Derek Reeves, our centre forward, got four of the goals and I actually ended up with the ball from the game. Derek had given it to the supporters club and one of the fans came to me one day, he was an older chap and he said '**I've got this ball, I've got no family and I'd love you to have it'**. It was very kind of him, the ball was signed by all of the team and I donated it to raise money for Ted's statue at the club."

### TERRY PAINE
"Terry was the kind of guy that if you were playing in a tight game, he was the one that was going to win. You knew he was just going to pop up with something special. An absolutely brilliant player, he never got injured like the rest of us and I always really appreciated what he could do. Terry was a real character and I've got nothing but great memories of him.

I think we complemented each other too, because opposition teams had two completely different types of wingers to deal with. Terry had his ball skills, trickery and the accuracy of his crossing. Whereas I was more of a pace guy, just running getting at them creating chances.

We always respected each other and I have great memories of him and hopefully he has some of me too. He's in South Africa now and I'm in Australia but we keep in touch."

### THE ATMOSPHERE INSIDE THE DELL
"It was always a very special atmosphere at The Dell, it was worth a goal a game at least to us. The fans were always fantastic too, even with 20,000 it felt like 40,000...it was just magical. Having been a part of it on the terraces as a kid and then being out there was wonderful. Of course there were the tough times as well, when things were going the other way and those days when you weren't having a great game.

There was always a lot of pressure at The Dell for both sides, but when we got those wins you could feel the fans joy and it was a pleasure to make them all happy, it was just fantastic."

### THANK YOU TO THE FANS
"I have just been amazed at the support I've had from the Saints supporters. I would just

like to thank every one of them for their ongoing commitment to the team, it means so much after all these years to be remembered. The day that I left The Dell I thought that would be it, nobody will know who I am in a few years. But I have been retired now for about fifty odd years and I really just want to say how much I appreciate all your thoughts and loyalty still to this day. It really does help to know that people care about you. So thank you."

# LIFE OF A SAINT

LIFE OF A SAINT

# TERRY PAINE
## M.B.E

1956 - 1974
**POSITION** : Winger
**APPS** : 812
**GOALS** : 187

**DEBUT**: 16/03/1957 v Brentford

**SAINTS HONOURS** : 1959 - 1960 Third Division Champion, 1965 - 1966 Second Division Runner Up, 1966 World Cup Winner

Part of the 1966 World Cup England squad, Terry Paine is our World Cup Winning Saint. Born in 1939 in Winchester, Terry signed amateur forms for Southampton in 1956 before making his professional debut in 1957. He would go on to make a record number of appearances for the Saints and score 160 goals.

A career spanning eighteen seasons saw him part of the 1959 - 1960 side which won promotion to the Second Division. In 1966, not only was he part of Sir Alf Ramsey's England squad who lifted the Jules Rimet, he also helped Saints to secure promotion to the First Division for the first time. Teaming up with John Sydenham he was part of the formidable duo of wingers that would strike fear into any opposition.

### WINCHESTER BOY BECOMES A SAINT
"I started playing at a young age for a local side called Hythe Corinthians and then moved to Winchester City in the Hampshire League. At the time, it was run by a former Saint Harry Osman and if you look him up you'll see that he was the top goal scorer for a winger...until I beat his record.

My father was a welder for the British Railways and in those days you were looking to get yourself a trade. So he got me into the British Railways works at Eastleigh where I served a year in the office and then took up my apprenticeship to be a coach builder.

While I was working there, there was a fanatic Saints fan and he heard that I was going up to Arsenal for a trial...in fact I went up twice. When he heard this he dropped Ted Bates a note to say I was going to Arsenal and he should take a look at me. Harry Osman had also been on the phone to Ted. I was in demand and I also had a trial at Portsmouth. Arsenal sent me a letter to say that they wanted me to go up for a final trial and my understanding was that the assistant to Tom Whittaker, who was one the most famous Arsenal Managers, forgot to send me forms to sign for Arsenal ahead of that final trail.

In the meantime, Ted Bates had got myself and Colin Holmes, who also worked with me at the railways, into the office at The Dell and locked the door. He wouldn't let us out until we signed forms and we kept saying that we had been invited to go to Arsenal and he said **'You don't want to go there!'** Now, by this point I was really hungry and wanted to get home so I signed the forms. In those days once you signed a form that was it you belonged to the club and that's how my journey with Southampton began."

## TED BATES BUILDING THE FOUNDATIONS
"Ted Bates was the man who put in the foundations for the club at the time. He introduced the youth team and managed to get a former Saints, Spurs and Welsh international called Ernie Jones to coach the side. We got through to the Semi-Final of the Youth Cup and we were the first team to beat the Busby Babes at Old Trafford. We won 3-2 although we had lost the game at The Dell (I think we lost 5-3 after the two games). At full time at Old Trafford Sir Matt Busby came into the dressing rooms to congratulate us on being one of the greatest youth teams he had seen. It was a great young side and out of that group about seventeen or eighteen of us turned professional.

Ted really gave me the confidence to play because he had so much trust in me. When I signed to Southampton we were in the Third Division and there was no hurry in those days, not like there is today where it all has to be instant success.

We were given time to develop as players and Ted built his Southampton side on the foundations of that youth team. He signed Jimmy Shield for £1,000 and the money came from the supporters club and when we secured promotion in the 1959-60 season he then built again, which enabled us to get promoted further in 1966.

One memory I hold dear is that I scored the last goal in the Second Division away at Leyton Orient to get us promoted. We finished second that year and went up with Manchester City. Ironically, we then played against Manchester City in our first game in the First Division and I scored the goal there to get us a 1-1 draw. So I scored the last goal in Second Division and the first in the First Division for the Saints.

I've got so much admiration for Ted Bates and what he did for the club and obviously the length of time he served the club as well. Nobody is ever going to do that again."

## PAINE MAKES HIS DEBUT v BRENTFORD

"I was playing in the youth team and I was still working at British Railways at the time. When I signed pro I played one game for the Southampton A side against Cowes in the Isle of Wight, the next week I played in the reserves and then the week after I phoned Ted to ask where I was playing that coming Saturday and he told me I was in the first team.

I remember the game well...we drew 3-3 v Brentford and I played outside left. At the time I played outside right but for that game I was on the left. I was naturally right footed but could also use my left foot.

That match was a week before my eighteenth birthday. The following weekend I was in the side again and I scored my first goal which was on my birthday weekend against Aldershot and we drew the game 1-1.

I remember after that game Ted came to my house to speak with my mum and dad to say I could transfer my apprenticeship to a company called CPC which was affiliated to the club through the youth set up. Dad insisted that I had a trade and that was the only way to get him to agree to let me go full time at the club. The irony was I never even set foot inside CPC and I couldn't even tell you where it was!"

## NO NATIONAL SERVICE FOR PAINE

"At the time, we also had National Service and we had to go down to the Army Centre to sign up and be examined to make sure we were fit to serve. I found out that if you had bad ears you could get out of it. So I went in to see the hearing specialist and he said **'Oh I see you have put on here bad ears, stand over there by the window'**. So I faced away from him and I could hear him saying a few things but I didn't say anything back. He said **'Oh my you have got bad ears'** and sent me to Winchester hospital to get a final check.

I walked into the specialist at Winchester Hospital and the doctor said **'Terry what are you doing here?'** So I explained and he signed me off and I managed to get out of doing National Service. I felt a bit bad because John Sydenham had already gone and was expecting me to join him."

## 1965 - 1966 PAINE, SYDENHAM & CHIVERS

"That was a pretty special season. Martin Chivers emerged on the scene and that allowed our top goal scorer at the time, George O'Brien, the move to Leyton Orient. George had been phenomenal in scoring goals for Southampton, his record is second to none but his time had come to move on.

Martin came in and he was big, strong, very quick and he really fed on the service that John and I were able to give him. I scored twenty or so goals that season too, so it was a really good combination in front of goal with his thirty goals.

We had a really good side and as we progressed through that season it dawned on us that we really had a chance of getting promotion, which would have been the first time in the club's history that they would have been in the First Division.

Everybody kept comparing us to the side in 1949-1950. Back then, the Saints were eight points clear and in the end they missed out by one point. Everyone said they didn't want to go up and they blew it on purpose, but in truth their top goal scorer was injured and they dropped a lot of points in those games he was amiss. So that was floating around in the background, but it didn't affect us. We had a great side, full of confidence and we could score goals but also defend.

The relationship with John and Martin came quite naturally. John and I had been playing together for a while and we knew what we could do and were confident in the way we played. It was just a case of Martin coming in to fit into that and he did that so well, he was a tremendous finisher. It was sad when he left, as he didn't spend too much time with us before he moved to Tottenham."

## TOTTENHAM AFTER PAINE

"Tottenham chased me all my life, they were waiting at every away game asking if I had handed in a transfer request yet. A fella called Harry Evans, who was Bill Nicholson's right hand man, was always there waiting outside grounds to ask me if I was going to move.

There were a lot of rumours about me leaving all the time and a lot of it was tongue in cheek from my point of view. In those days we weren't getting paid very much so there was a guy who worked for the People Newspaper. Every so often you would see a story: **'Terry Paine wants a transfer'** and he would give me £50.00 for the story and then I would deny it on the Monday. It did get to a point where it was getting a little bit serious if I would move or not, but Ted Bates never mentioned to me whether or not a team ever came in for me."

## PAINES PERFECT VISION

"I practiced a lot but something I naturally had was my vision. I saw things very early on. I would talk to Ted Bates about it and he would say **'How do you do it?'** In all honesty it just came naturally but it was like taking a photograph before the ball arrived. I could just see what was going to happen next.

I already had a picture in my mind of what was going to happen. George O'Brien once said I could play the game sitting in the stand because I saw so much and used to see it so quickly. Of course then you had to produce it and give the final ball and put players in the game.

I don't know what year it was but Ted Bates decided to have someone in the stand marking us and collecting stats. I happened to see this guy after we had scored twenty one goals during the time and he said **'Terry did you know you scored or assisted nineteen of the twenty one goals?'** and I thought **'That's not a bad record!'"**

## PARTNERSHIPS
"I had some great partnerships during my time at Southampton. Derek Reeves in the early days was one. He was our top goal scorer in the league and he scored 145 goals for the club. George O'Brien then came in after him and I had a great relationship on the field with the great Ron Davies. That partnership was one that would catch most people's eyes.

Ron Davis was probably the best footballer I've ever seen in my life in the game of football. When you played the ball in for him you knew that he was going to be on the end of it. He was a tremendous player.

In the later stages of my career when I dropped back more into the midfield it was telepathic between myself and Mick Channon. I didn't have to look and he didn't have to worry. When he went on a run he knew I was going to get it and put him in. We were a fair old combination in those days."

## OUR SAINT BECOMES ONE OF THE THREE LIONS
"I believe I got picked for England when I caught Sir Alf Ramsey's eye when he was the Manager at Ipswich. He came to The Dell with a very good side which clinched promotion that year. We played them in the FA Cup and we beat them 7-1, I scored a couple of goals that day and I think that stayed in his memory.

Apart from your first international, which for me was against Czechoslovakia, my next best moment was playing against the best team ever picked to play against England. It was a Rest of the World side in 1963 and I scored the first goal and Jimmy Greaves got the winner. We beat them 2-1 and Denis Law scored the goal for them, their side was full of greats including: Alfredo di Stéfano, Eusébio, Karl-Heinz Schnellinger and Ferenc Puskás to name a few. It was an unbelievable team that we beat on that day and a very special memory for me.

Another game that sticks in my mind was a match against West Germany which was played in 1965, one year before the 1966 final. The team that lined up against us was pretty much the same side we faced in the final. On that day, I scored the goal in a 1-0 victory in Nuremberg... again another day I won't forget."

### 16th JULY 1966 ENGLAND v MEXICO & OUR WORLD CUP WINNING SAINT

"When it came to 1966 you have to remember that I was a Second Division player, funnily enough I never played for England as a First Division player because after 1966 Sir Alf never picked me again. But having only played Second Division whenever I played for England, I had to step up not one, but two steps to match the international level of my team mates like Bobby Moore, Bobby Charlton and Gordon Banks who played in the First Division.

After the game against Uruguay, which we drew 0-0, we had a team meeting and in that meeting Sir Alf Ramsey announced the team for the Mexico match. He read my name and as I came out of that meeting I thought **'Wow I'm going to be playing in a World Cup finals. This will be a moment to treasure!'**

Then to go on to win 2-0 at Wembley was incredible and in front of 92,570 fans. I got a bang on the head in the game and was concussed pretty much throughout. Which means I can't really remember much. The problem with getting that knock was that I was about to miss out going forward. Sir Alf was one of those Managers that if you got a knock on the head he wouldn't gamble. I remember a couple of years ago one of the England players said **'What would have happened if Terry hadn't got concussed? Would he have played the next game?'** Who knows, maybe Sir Alf had a plan anyway that didn't feature me going forward as we were called the wingless wonders. I was just very honoured to have played my part.

Winning the World Cup was a very special moment in my career. On the day of the final you have to remember there were no substitutes, so those of us who weren't involved had to sit in the stand. Sir Alf had told us five minutes before the end of the game to come down and be there in the tunnel. As we got down West Germany equalised, so I have got photographs of us all sat down on the red carpet watching the extra time.

Being part of that history was incredible, but I also really felt for Sir Alf Ramsey, because he had put his head on the block two years before saying we would win, which was a pretty lofty statement."

### PAINE GETS HIS MEDAL - 10 JUNE 2009
"On the day of the final only the players who played got a medal. Many years later, one of the national papers ran a campaign to get medals for all those players who were in the side but didn't feature in the final. It was a brilliant day, we all met up and went to Number 10 Downing Street and got our medals from the Prime Minister. We then went to Wembley to watch England play that night and we were guests of honour."

### THE DELL THE HOME OF A SAINT
"When you say it became your home it really did. The beauty of it was the closeness of all the supporters. In the bigger games the atmosphere was electric and teams wouldn't like to come to The Dell, simple as that. It became a fortress for us and an opponent wouldn't have wanted to come to The Dell needing points to stay up.

I remember an FA Cup tie v Nottingham Forest and it was one of those absolutely electric days. It was 1963 and we were in the Second Division and they were in the First. With fourteen minutes to go we were 3-0 down. The fans were right behind us and we came back to draw 3-3, taking the game to a second replay at White Hart Lane."

### 1974 PAINE MOVES ON
"At that time there was a change in personnel; Ted Bates had moved up stairs and Lawrie McMenemy had come in. When you look back on things you can understand why he let me go when he did. I was a strong personality in the dressing room I don't deny that, having been Captain for about ten years. At the time, it came as a huge disappointment, mainly because it was my testimonial year but things move on and so did I. John Sillett had got the job at Hereford United and he was a former Southampton lad and I knew him and his brother Peter from their time at Chelsea. John became an extraordinary coach and I just happened to pick the phone up to say congratulations on the job. **'Best of luck'** I said and

'**By the way I have got a free transfer**'. To which he asked me if I would come to Hereford and be his assistant. My playing days weren't over and I went on to play another 111 league games."

## A THANK YOU FROM OUR WORLD CUP WINNING SAINT
"They sing **'He's one of their own'** and I certainly was one of their own for many many years and I really appreciated all of the support from the fans over the years. I was very lucky to have tremendous support from the supporters of Southampton.

I have made many friends and acquaintances over the years and it's nice now having the Saints Archive page on Facebook. It's lovely to see the memories and photos that come in. It is great to see it all being shared and I chip in now and again.

I really do love being in touch with everyone and people are so nice to me. So thank you, they say once you're a Saint you are always a Saint and that's certainly true in my case."

# LIFE OF A SAINT

# FRANCIS BENALI
## M.B.E

1988 - 2003
POSITION : Defender
APPS : 321
GOALS : 1

**DEBUT:** 01/10/1988 v Derby County

**SAINTS HONOURS :** 1992 Zenith Data Cup Runner Up, 2003 FA Cup Final Runner Up

Southampton born and bred, Francis Benali began his career in youth football playing for Windsor United in the Tyro League. In his youth Francis Benali was a prolific striker and soon caught the eye of the Saints in 1985. Benali signed his first professional contract in 1988 and quickly established himself in the Saints squad under the management of Chris Nicholl.

Considering his goal scoring ability as a youth player, Benali only found the back of the net once, it came in a game v Leicester City at the Dell, converting a free kick from Matthew Le Tissier. Benali spent a brief time on loan at Nottingham Forest in 2001 before playing his last game for Southampton FC in 2004. He then had a brief spell at Eastleigh in the Non-League playing twenty two games for the Spitfire's between 2006 and 2008. Since hanging up his boots Francis Benali has taken on three major challenges for Cancer Research UK raising over £1,000,000.

**SOUTHAMPTON BORN BENALI ALWAYS A SAINT**
"I remember being a young schoolboy when we had our big moment and won the FA Cup in 1976. I went to school in Archers Road at Bannister First School which was just a stones

throw from The Dell. I was convinced that the bus was going to go past our school on the parade and I remember when it didn't I was really disappointed that I didn't actually get to see all the players with the cup. I had family in Liverpool so as I grew up I followed Southampton and Liverpool but as I got older Southampton became my only team.

Walking past The Dell on the way to and from school every day as well was a real big part of my life even as a young boy. I always loved playing football, then over time it became a little bit more serious and I started playing for a few teams when I became a teenager."

## FRANNY BECOMES A SAINT

"It happened really really quickly because football, as it was for many kids back then, was just playing in the park, in the playground or in the streets with your mates really. It wasn't until I was thirteen that I played for a proper organised team, Winsor United in the Tyro League. I was playing for my middle school at the Sports Centre and one of the Winsor United Managers was watching. He came over and had a chat and asked me if I played for any other teams. I said **'No'** as I just played with my mates in the school team. He then invited me to go along and have a few training sessions and naturally because I loved football, I said yes. I was thirteen at the time and within that first year of playing for Winsor I had signed associate schoolboy forms for Southampton.

I got spotted by the scouting network at the club and I was invited to go along and do some training sessions at The Dell and that was the start of the journey on a formal basis with the football club.

When I signed as associate schoolboy I remember we got taken into the dressing room on a match day to have a picture, I think it was taken by the Echo. I have vivid memories of being sat there with Greg Llewellyn and I remember Danny Wallace being there and Rueben Agboola and just thinking **'Wow this is amazing!'** That atmosphere and buzz in the dressing room on a match day just fueled my desire to want to keep progressing, keep improving and hopefully getting to be in that dressing room one day as a Southampton first team player."

## SIGNING PRO

"All I wanted to do was become a professional footballer, so signing that contract was very much me achieving that goal. I turned pro at eighteen years old and Chris Nicholl was Manager.

Lawrie McMenemy signed me as a schoolboy, but by the time I'd come through the ranks he had moved on and it was Chris who offered me that first contract. It was an amazing moment when I realised I had done it and reached that goal I had always dreamt of, but realising at the same time it was only the first rung of the ladder and once you were on you had to start climbing to earn your place in the first team.

It was a very proud moment. I'd gone from earning a YTS wage to earning £100.00 a week in my first pro contract. There was no discussion, there was no negotiation, Chris Nicholl just said **'There's the offer take it or leave it.'** He said **'Keep improving, break into the first team and we'll sit down and talk about new terms.'**

Naturally I signed it straight away and he was good to his word, I broke in the first team and he sat me down to sign a new improved contract."

## THE DEBUT v DERBY COUNTY

"I'd gone through a transition of going from a striker in my youth team days, to being a midfielder at this point. I think it's fair to say I even had a few disciplinary issues back then and the club felt I would be better suited to the midfield and that's where I made my debut.

I was on the bench for the game v Derby County at The Dell. I remember thinking **'Right this is it, this is what you have wanted to do for all these years'**. Obviously when you're breaking in and make your debut and you go in and out of the team and that was a frustrating time, but it certainly gave me a determination to play more and establish myself in the side.

The game itself seemed to go by in a flash. I came off the bench to replace Kevin Moore and we drew 0-0. I remember relishing it and loving every moment. The one thing that did stick out in that game was how different it was compared to youth team and reserve team football."

## THE DELL

"I've always told people it was home to me, it was somewhere that I knew every inch of. It was just so familiar and it was a benefit to us as a team over the years looking back throughout my career. The atmosphere there at times could be electric. The supporters were in such close proximity, within touching distance of the pitch which made it a very hostile place for visiting players and teams to come to.

If it was a game under lights then it took it to a different level. The atmosphere and feel to it at a night game was special, under the floodlights it felt almost magical.

I remember being there as a schoolboy stood in the terraces watching and almost being swayed around in the crowd and then that little bit, that surge when something was about to happen which is an experience you don't get in all seater stadiums.

When I first broke through it would have been all terracing. So we would have crowds of 30,000 and to have the capacity of St Mary's squeezed into The Dell you can imagine how that felt and sounded.

It was a great place to play; obviously football moves on and you need these modern stadiums for many reasons, but I have a real soft spot for The Dell."

## THE LAST GOODBYE - SOUTHAMPTON v ARSENAL 19th May 2001

"That last day was almost like saying goodbye to a family member in a way. The Dell had been such a big part of my life for so many years and I knew the new stadium was there and we had to make a move in order to progress as a football club. Don't get me wrong it was an exciting time, but it was also tinged with that sadness of having to leave The Dell behind. I think for players like myself and Matt and the supporters that had been going there for many years, it had just been such a big part of our lives. It was a huge part of our community and the city.

To go into a game knowing that this was the last competitive match there, was quite special and unique and the way it all turned out with us winning and Matt scoring the final goal the way he did, I guess it couldn't have been written any better.

Stuart Gray was very good to me and Matt. He spoke to us in the week before the game and said that we both would be on the pitch at some stage of the game. So that mentally prepared me for it and I was so grateful to have that opportunity to have been out there in such a special game.

For Matt to have done what he did and the reaction of the crowd was incredible, also being in that dressing room for the last time on a competitive day was very special.

Then of course the final match v Brighton, I remember the supporters being on the pitch ripping seats out and taking whatever they could as a little memento. Pieces of turf, toilet signs, whatever they could get their hands on.

It was a day that anyone who was there will never ever forget."

## BENALI MOVES TO FOREST

"It was very difficult and strange. There were lots of feelings and emotions at the time and I remember sitting down with Karen and the children, Luke and Kenzie, who were obviously a lot younger then, but it was a massive dilemma for me. I knew professionally I was at an age where there was a lot of football left in me. Glenn Hoddle made it clear at the time that I wasn't part of his plans. I thought **'Blimey you know what, I don't want to leave, I want to stay here, but if this is how it's going to be I've got to consider a move'**.

The city and the club had been our lives and all of a sudden there's a situation from a career perspective that was now potentially affecting us as a family, it was very difficult. I knew I had to make that move in a way, so I thought initially **'Let's get a loan move and let's get playing'**.

There were a number of clubs that came in for me and geographically Nottingham obviously was not the closest. There were clubs that were nearer that were interested in signing me and from a family perspective and travel it would have made things a lot easier. But I had a chat with David Platt who was Manager at Forest at the time, knowing what he was doing and the history of that club, I felt it was the right place to go. Looking back on it now it was a very good experience for me, I think it grew me as a player and as a person.

I had always been the local boy welcoming players to my hometown club and all of a sudden I'm the new boy in a new dressing room with only one or two familiar faces which included Dave Beasant. Being in that position grew me as a player and a character.

I was commuting two and a half hours there and back every day as I didn't want to be stuck in hotels on my own. If we finished at lunchtime I knew I could be back home by five o'clock and be with the family. That was a slog for three months doing that up and down the Motorway, it was hard.

I enjoyed my three months there and I guess it couldn't have worked out any better for me. By the time the loan finished, Hoddle went to Spurs and that opened the door for me to come back. I was really happy it worked out like that, because I never really wanted to leave.

Some people say **'You're not a one club man'** because of the 15 games I played at Forest. I guess technically that is true, but I've never seen myself anything other than a one club person."

## THAT GOAL v LEICESTER

"I'm pleased I got at least one goal because obviously I came to the club as a striker. Over time it didn't play on my mind, but if I got myself in a certain position it would be like **'Right this could be the moment where I could potentially score'**. Obviously the supporters became fully aware of that and the odds on me scoring the first goal went crazy each week, I think a lot people probably lost a lot more money on me over the years.

It was a magical moment when it came along, a real highlight in my career looking back on it. I was pleased that it came at The Dell as it probably wouldn't have had quite the same impact if I had done it away from home. It meant something on the day as well, it was a very close game with Leicester. I think Matt scored our other goal and Robbie Savage scored for the Foxes. To score the winner on the day in front of all the supporters that had been so good to me over the years was brilliant.

Over the year I had ideas of goal celebrations and what I'd do if the goal eventually came and when it did happen that day I just remember there was almost a stunned silence.

The whole stadium just went quiet for a second or two and then it just erupted, I just remember standing there screaming and then next thing I knew the boys had piled on top of me."

## WHEN FRANNY SAW RED V WIMBLEDON

"Well I thought it was a little bit harsh to be honest. For anyone that remembers Wimbledon at the time they were a very physical and intimidating side and they played on that. They had Vinnie Jones and a few others that were almost like the ringleaders of the crazy gang.

You knew going to Plow Lane that you were going to be in for a physically and mentally challenging game. We had players in the side that relished the physical challenge and we had a mentality that we had got to stand up to this. It's almost like meeting fire with fire.

I overstepped the line that day, I think there had been a few incidents going on beforehand. John Fashanu was an outspoken character as well and he was quite vocal during the game. I had a thought in my mind that next chance I get I'm going to try and put in a stern challenge and leave something on him.

I think it was slightly mistimed, but it was pretty spectacular the way he catapulted over me. Obviously there was the initial red mist but that quickly turned into the reality of I could have potentially cost the team some points and put pressure on them as a group of players without me being on the pitch.

I know Matt loves it because we were losing 3-1 and when I got sent off and we ended up drawing 3-3 and he scored a hat-trick. So he loves the fact that I got sent off when we were losing and they salvaged a point without me being on the pitch."

## TEAMMATES

"I have to say I'm really honoured and privileged to have played with so many incredible footballers but also so many lovely people as well. Matt Le Tissier is one where we just connected and bonded straight away. It's a friendship that's just gone from strength to strength over the years. I think largely that's down what we experienced together as players. Those experiences where as a team we faced adversity and struggled trying to survive. I know Matt took it upon his shoulders personally to be the player that was going to score the goals that would ultimately mean our survival. From a friend and a teammate's perspective I could see his qualities and as a team we knew he was the star. Players of my calibre and style of play would willingly run, tackle and do what we had to do to enable Matt to create his piece of magic to get us a win.

There was some great senior pros when I came through. The dressing room was littered with international players like Peter Shilton and Joe Jordan. You also had players who came through like I was trying to do like Nick Holmes. He was an incredible professional and person. He was somebody that was just so generous with his time and advice.

It was a tough school to be in when we were kids coming through, but at the same time there was a real warmth from those players as well. Jimmy Case was senior pro for many years and you had to earn the right to be in that first team group, but once you did and you showed that you had the qualities to be in that arena you were very much welcomed in. I think that's why probably not just myself but a lot of players came through the system in that era, that was a great environment to be in.

Flip it to Wayne Bridge for example, here was a youngster that I knew was my competition for a place in the team. Yet I couldn't not offer my advice or encouragement to him as a young player. I saw that as my responsibility not just as a team member but as club Captain at the time. For me as a person it was only right to give that back to the younger players coming through albeit ultimately he did take the place in the side."

## 2003 FA CUP FINAL

"It was an incredible journey. Despite all the efforts through the years to try and replicate what the boys of 1976 did it's a real shame that we came so close in 2003, but couldn't quite do it.

We had a wonderful group of players and the management were great. There was a belief and confidence in the squad that even if we went behind in the game we could get back into it. Gordon Strachan and his team pushed us hard every single day, we had the quality and the mindset of a group at the time, that ultimately meant we had a team capable of beating anyone on our day.

We got to the final and I remember that day being just as I dreamt it would be apart from not winning it. Which does take the shine off it somewhat, missing that extra step to have lifted the trophy.

The supporters on the day were absolutely incredible, that sea of yellow and blue was amazing. As a player coming out of the tunnel and seeing the thousands and thousands of supporters still there, even after the final whistle had gone. The Arsenal fans had pretty much all gone and to see our fans still packed in half an hour after full time was incredible.

I played twice en route to the final, in both the Millwall games when Wayne Bridge was out injured. I was pleased to have played a small part of the journey but it was tinged with a bit of disappointment from a professional perspective that I wasn't part of the starting eleven on the day or on the bench. At the same time though Gordon Strachan was very good to me and kept me in and around the squad. Hopefully I offered something even off the pitch when I wasn't playing to the group.

At full time Danny Higginbotham held his medal out to me and said **'You deserve this more than I do, you are a Southampton man'**. I always say to him it would have been interesting to see if he would have offered it to me if it had been a winner's medal. I couldn't take it though and I said to him **'No that's yours'**. It turned out I did get a medal as the club asked for a few more for those players who were part of the journey but didn't feature in the final."

## THE FANS

"I had a number of fans to win over, shall we say, over the years like every player does I guess. You're not going to have everybody loving what you do and how you do it. I was never going to let that hold me back. My mindset that time was **'Ok I may not be the best player but you'll never be able to look at me and criticise me for giving less than 100%'**.

I think over the years people grew to respect that, even if they didn't like how I played they realised the qualities that I brought to the club and how I wanted to drive the team forward on a daily basis. I tried to set an example not just on a match day but also in training and also in how I lived my life personally. Hopefully I was an example to my teammates especially youngsters.

My relationship with the fans has been very special to me. I always felt very fortunate to be out on the pitch representing the club, the fans and the city. Having been a fan growing up I felt I was one of them out on the pitch. So the least I could do was give 100% game after game. Even if I had a bad game or made mistakes which happened quite often they would at least hopefully admire and respect me for the effort I put in and how I always played for the badge."

## MARATHON MAN - FRANCIS BENALI MBE

"The response from not only Saints fans but the wider football community has been amazing. Looking back on the support I have received personally from my family first and foremost, the support team, the local community and the football club has been incredible.

I couldn't have reached the fundraising target or probably even completed the challenges without that wider network of support. That is something that has always humbled me and made me eternally grateful because I couldn't have done it without everybody. So thank you to you all."

# PAUL JONES

1997 - 2004
POSITION : Goalkeeper
APPS : 220

DEBUT: 09/08/1997 v Bolton Wanderers

SAINTS HONOURS : 1997-1998 Player of the Year, 2003 FA Cup Final Runner Up

Paul Jones signed for Southampton in 1997 joining up with his former Stockport County manager Dave Jones. Paul made an instant impact winning the 1997 - 1998 Player of the Season award in his first year at the club, helping the team achieve a twelfth place finish in the Premier League. His performances that season also earned him a call up to the Wales squad where he established himself as the number one for his country making fifty appearances between 1997 and 2006.

Jones played his part in the 2003 FA Cup run playing in the semi final victory v Watford at Villa Park. Although he was on the bench for the final, he was the first ever goalkeeper to make an appearance as a substitute in an FA Cup Final when he came in the sixty sixth minute for the injured Antti Niemi. Paul joined Liverpool on loan in 2004 making two appearances before leaving the Saints to rejoin Wolves that January.

## FOOTBALL LEAGUE TO THE PREMIER LEAGUE

"I had played under Dave Jones at Stockport County the season before, so when he signed for Southampton he rang me and asked if I would like to come across to the Saints. It was a no brainer for me, not only because of the opportunity to work with Dave again but also the chance to play in the Premier League.

Joining the club was a big thing for me and I was really looking forward to it, they put me in the Hilton the night before and the next morning we went down to The Dell and had a look around. It was a great club and I signed on the dotted line.

It was really easy for me to settle in at the club, players like Matt Le Tissier, Francis Benali and Jason Dodd were brilliant. There was a great dressing room, Matt was obviously the star of the team, but he was down to earth just like he is now and was very easy to get on with. They all made me feel very welcome. I signed just before we went away on a pre-season tour so that was a great opportunity for me to get to know everyone as you're in each other's pockets twenty four seven."

## 1997 - 1998 FIRST SEASON PLAYER OF THE YEAR

"I really enjoyed my first season with Southampton and we finished twelfth that year. I had a good season and my form followed on from the previous season I had at Stockport, I had also won Player of the Year there too in my final season with them. It was great to win the award as it was really nice to be recognised by the fans. So to get that recognition in my first season at Saints was brilliant."

## THE DELL

"With 15,000 in there it felt more like 30,000. The atmosphere and the fans being so close to you was brilliant. I liked the tight grounds where the fans were on top of you because it created a much better atmosphere, but one of the best things for us players, apart from the fans was the pitch, it was always very good. The guys working behind the scenes and all the ground staff were fantastic. So add that to the atmosphere and it made The Dell a very special place."

## SOUTHAMPTON v ARSENAL SETTING UP LE GOD

"I would be lying if I said I was trying to pick Matt out. I was just trying to get the ball into the box to see what happened. I had a free kick just outside my area and got it up there, it got a knock down and then Matt took his touch and banged it in. It was a fitting end to say goodbye to The Dell and if you were writing a script for that day that was how you would have written it."

## JONES ESTABLISHES HIMSELF AT THE WELSH NO.1
"I had gotten my first call up in the summer just before I signed for Southampton for a friendly v Scotland. Once I started playing for Saints I took over from Neville Southall pretty much from the October of my first season. I had only been in two squads before that which was the Scotland game and then a trip away to Turkey.

It was a whirlwind time, joining Southampton playing in the Premier League and then getting the regular call up and taking over from one of my heroes in Southall. Following in his footsteps was very special as I had big gloves to fill. I went on be the number one for ten years and make fifty appearances for my country was very special to me."

## ON LOAN TO LIVERPOOL
"I grew up as a Liverpool fan and at the time I wasn't starting for Southampton, Antti Niemi was playing at the time. I had been training on Thursday, I got back home and I got a call from Gordon Strachan. He said **'Liverpool have come, in do you fancy a loan move?'** So I said why not and then Gérard Houllier gave me a call.

I drove up that night, trained with the squad on the Friday and then played against Aston Villa on the Saturday, so it all happened pretty quickly. I had obviously played at Anfield many times with Southampton, but also with the Wales squad as we played there when the Millennium Stadium was being built. But to go out in the Liverpool shirt and touch the 'This is Anfield' sign which I hadn't done before (as I always felt you had to be a Liverpool player to do that) made it a special memory for me; having the chance to play for the club I supported as a kid was pretty awesome. We beat Villa 1-0 and I kept a clean sheet in front of the Kop. I played one more game before I came back and eventually moved to Wolves."

## 2003 FA CUP
"The Semi-Final was fantastic. It was a game you certainly didn't want to lose as you were so close to the final. With Brett Ormerod scoring and then of course us getting the winner

via the own goal, it was a great performance and the fans were incredible. They were exactly the same at the final at Cardiff too with that sea of yellow and blue.

From a personal point of view the final was disappointing for me. Antti Niemi came back in and he wasn't really fit, he lasted about sixty minutes before I came on. I was disappointed not to be starting especially as it was in Cardiff. I would say that was one of the biggest disappointments in my career, although I came on and picked up the stats of being the first keeper to come on as a substitute in an FA Cup Final and also the only keeper to lose an FA Cup final having not conceded a goal. Not necessarily stats you want, as I would rather have played and got a winners medal, but I suppose it makes a good quiz question. When I look back though I can still say I played in and FA Cup Final."

## TEAM MORALE
"In those early years we had such a good team morale, the players were brilliant. We had a set of lads who I wouldn't say that we were world beaters but we pulled together, we worked hard. We were a team of good honest hard working lads and when you have that you can do well in the league, get results and that's what we did.

I remember in my second season it went down to the wire a little bit but we stayed up by five points in the end. At the time it was pretty tight but that was the only season I was there when it got pretty close to going down."

# JASON DODD

1989 - 2005
**POSITION** : Defender
**APPS** : 453
**GOALS:** 13

**DEBUT:** 03/10/1989 v York

**SAINTS HONOURS** : 2003 FA Cup Final Runner Up

Signing for Southampton in 1989 from Bath City, Jason Dodd went on to captain the Saints and make 398 appearances scoring nine goals. He was part of a team that fought off relegation and his leadership qualities certainly helped secure safety on several occasions.

After retiring from playing, Jason Dodd returned to Southampton in 2007 to work as first team coach under George Burley and after Burley's departure he briefly took over as caretaker manager until the appointment of Nigel Pearson. In 2009 he returned as Director and Head Coach of the Youth academy, a role which he held until 2014.

## BATH CITY TO SOUTHAMPTON

"A year or two before I joined the Saints I became one of the first Non-League players to sign on a YTS. I signed with Bath City, who were in what is now the National League. There were four of us who were signed and on Monday, Wednesday and Friday we would train together and go to college, then we used to train on a Tuesday and Thursday evenings with the first team and play on Saturdays.

After about six months or so I realised that the YTS wasn't for me. At this point the club were quite smart and decided that I would go and work for them in the commercial department as assistant commercial manager. Which meant I was making cups of tea and going around delivering scratch cards to sell in local pubs. I had a little bubble car with Bath City printed all over it and I would deliver the cards. A couple of weeks later I would then go around and collect all the money. We shared the ground with Bristol Rovers so I used to work the turnstiles when they played at home too which kept me busy.

I was really enjoying playing at Bath and had got myself into the first team. There was a Southampton scout called Rod Ruddock who covered the area, he saw me play and spoke to Chris Nicholl about me and said '**You need to get this lad to come down to Southampton so you can have a look**'.

It was quite tough for me because I obviously had a job and Saints wanted me to go down from a months trial. I had to say to Bath that '**I'm going to give this a go**' because I didn't want to look back and say '**What if?**'

I came down and stayed with a lovely couple called Lynne and Gus who lived just up the road from The Dell. They were wonderful people that really looked after me. I was a bit of a mummy's boy so it was tough for me being away from home. I had never been away before, but they made it so comfortable for me and that really helped me settle in.

I would walk down to The Dell in the mornings and then we would get a minibus over to Wellington to train. I was given a first team pro to look after and I had Barry Horne. Being at a professional club was a real eye opener for me but I loved it. I was more or less getting home every night sleeping for twelve hours and then getting up and cranking on. After the four weeks they said they wanted me to stay for another two.

Dave Merrington was the youth team manager, he was an amazing man for us lads and you can tell that by the way we all still speak about him now. It wasn't just the football, he taught us life skills. He was immense for us and I was lucky to have someone who was firm but really fair and it was no wonder why so many boys went on to have careers. Not just at Southampton but all over and that was down to Dave being such an amazing coach for us.

On Fridays we had jobs to do at The Dell, from cleaning the away team dressing room to the toilets. It would get to 4pm and we would be waiting to go and Dave would be going around checking what we had done. Many a times we had to get our kit back on and do laps around the pitch because we hadn't done a good enough job, he would make us do twenty laps and we would have a game the next day too. It was all about working together and it made us not just better players but better people as well.

I remember when he used to drive the minibus to take us to games on a Saturday morning. After about one or two trips you learned not to talk to Dave when he was driving, because he would be up the front and someone would ask him a question and he would turn around while driving to talk to us and we would be wetting ourselves shouting; **'Dave Look at the road!'**.

After the six weeks I was then told by Chris Nicholl that they were going to give me a contract, but they couldn't do anything until they had told the rest of the scholars what was happening to them. There was about ten of them and they didn't really like me, because I had come in and got a contract after six weeks when they had been there for five or six years. So I wasn't best liked but you look back now and can understand why.

When they were told about their contract it was horrendous. We were all in the dressing room, one person would be standing in the corridor and one person would be in the office with the boss. He would be telling them if it was a yes or no.

Chris offered me a one year contract and I managed to get in and around the first team squad fairly quickly in the summer of 1989-1990."

## THE DEBUT

"When it got to October we had a cup game v York, I came on for Raymond Wallace with about ten minutes to go. It was the longest ten minutes of my life. I couldn't breathe I was running around so much. After the game I thought that I would be off the bench here and there. So on the Saturday when we were at QPR playing away, I was on the coach keeping myself to myself, thinking I would just be on the bench, then in the dressing room the Manager named the team and I was starting. In the game I gave away a penalty, which luckily for me Tim Flowers saved and we won 4-1.

The following Saturday we were at home to Liverpool, now they had won the FA Cup the year before and only missed out on the title by goal difference, they were a good side so I was expecting Raymond Wallace to come back into the starting lineup. We were sat in the dressing room and at quarter to two I got told I was starting. I was about to make my full home debut v Liverpool.

I was so nervous, but managed to settle my nerves and I set up the first goal for Paul Rideout. It was a great result for us winning 4-1, the only thing I can really remember from that match is John Barnes. He was one of the best players in the world and we had just won and he came up to me and said '**Jason you played really well today!**' and that stuck with me forever. Firstly he knew my name and secondly they had been beaten and he had the decency to come up to me and say that. He didn't have to do that so it meant a lot.

I was very lucky and played twenty odd games that season and we finished seventh. I learnt so much in that first season from Chris Nicholl with him having been a former defender. I was learning all the time from senior pros like Glenn Cockerill, Micky Adams and Russell Osman and these players were amazing to me. The side had a great set of young players too with Le Tissier, Rodney and Raymond; the balance in the side was perfect.

For the first two years of my career I just watched and learned. I was very lucky to be part of a team where the senior professionals took the young lads under their wing."

## MOVING OUT OF THE DIGS
"As I said before, I was a bit of a mummy's boy and I was very homesick, but the club was very good with us young players. The host families they put us with were brilliant. Lynne and Gus who looked after me were magnificent. I only had to get out because they looked after me too well!

In the morning there was breakfast all laid out ready. I would get back from training and before I knew it my kit was washed and ready for the next day. Dinner was always on the table and they wouldn't even let me wash up. I was very lucky that I was with Lynne and Gus, it was their home and they had a family too with Candice and Little Gus but I had to get out because it was way too easy."

## RALLYING TOGEHTER

"At The Dell it wasn't just about the players, it was about the fans too. They were part of the team. They would throw the balls back to you, they were side by side with you when you took throw ins and a lot of the opposition didn't like that which played into our hands.

It was a massive advantage, because if you were to write two sides down side by side, we had good players but we were playing world class players at times. You would look at games and think for a Liverpool or Manchester United that a game v Southampton would be a walk in the park for them, but we had The Dell, we had that togetherness.

As players we also had that togetherness, we would go and have a round of golf or a couple of beers together and there wouldn't just be one or two of us there would be sixteen or eighteen of us. We were like a family, we would socialise together, we were comfortable around each other and we all knew each other's families.

We had to be like that for us to get out of trouble a few times when we were in real trouble. We had a roll up our selves up and let's do this together mentality. We wanted to play and we wanted to work hard for each other and that, mixed with the fans and The Dell, all worked in our favour.

For me, if the supporters see you giving everything, but you lose the game, of course they are disappointed, but they aren't going away saying **'Our players could have worked harder'**. They go away thinking the opposition were just a bit better than us today. Now if we did slack off, rightly so we used to get stick. People were paying good money to see us play and if we weren't putting in a shift we deserved the kick up the backside, but the players we had in that era would work hard. The Managers we had also knew that the togetherness was a big part of what would get us out of the dangers we got ourselves in.

The fans really were such a big part of it, I remember we had to go to Wimbledon one year and get a result, we needed to win. That day the supporters were incredible. The noise was frightening, we were up for it, they were up for it and that fired us up even more. On paper Wimbledon were the better side but we went and won 2-0."

## TEAMMATES

"For me, I very much got on with players like Neil Maddison and Tommy Widdrington who like me weren't stars of the show but when we were picking five-a-sides in training you had them in your team. Maybe we weren't as good as the world class players, but you knew what you were going to get from us. Those sorts of players I got on really well with because we had to work hard. We weren't a Matt Le Tissier, we didn't have the amazing skills he had, we had to work twice as hard. To be fair, with him playing in front of me I had to work three or four times as hard sometimes, but I would do that because he was that special he could win us games. So in theory, yes, he wouldn't track back sometimes, actually a lot of times and I would be overloaded, but I wouldn't moan about it because I knew one chance in a game and he would take it and win us the game. We had to work that bit harder to make sure we could get him the ball that little bit higher up the pitch so he could do the magic and we had the players to do that."

## SOUTHAMPTON v PORTSMOUTH

"I had a pretty good record v Portsmouth over the years when we played them. There weren't a lot of games but there were great matches to be involved in especially when we played them in the Premier League.

My first game v Portsmouth was at The Dell in the FA Cup in 1996 and for me it was the buildup that made it just as much as the game on the Saturday. It was everywhere you went, everyone was talking about it. Everyone wanted a ticket and that was always the first question I got about town. As a player on the match day itself you're focusing on your game but the atmosphere in that game was immense and it was a fantastic day.

I didn't score many goals so scoring against Portsmouth was very special. With the goal from the corner at St Mary's I should have gone a bit mental, but I was more interested in getting the team refocused and building on the goal. Also let be honest I couldn't go running off pretending I actually meant it.

They obviously took it off and gave it as an own goal but I still count it. I think that sticks in the supporters' memories too as it was a bit flukey but it was the first of three that got us the win that day."

## CAPTAIN DODD

"It was great for me and a real honour to captain Southampton. I had really good relationships with my Managers and they had a trust in me. I always had high standards, I was always on time, I always put in 100% and knew my strengths and limitations. I wasn't the best player but I was the player who would give everything and I grew up learning from some great captains and senior pros like Glenn Cockerill who I learned a lot from.

I always wanted to win and I would kick you up the backside to get what I wanted from you. I wouldn't have a go at you if you were just having a bad day, but if you were not picking up or doing your job I would. I also knew how to get best out of players and knew that Michael Svensson would need a different nudge than Claus would. It was understanding how all of the team ticked.

If there was a problem Managers could come to me and I would be honest. It was great for me and I had many years as Captain. I really enjoyed the off field responsibilities too, doing the interviews, going out to school and so on so I was very lucky to captain Southampton and really loved it."

## MANAGERS

"I was very lucky to work with some great Managers; for me, Gordon Strachan and Glenn Hoddle stand out, they were all about the small details that gave you that bit more.

With Glenn, I was on set plays and on Fridays if it wasn't going right he would just step in, zip the ball down, you didn't want him showing you up so it pushed you to be even better. He also brought in a lot of the psychology side of the game in too, which now is normal but back then it was all new.

When Gordon Strachan came in the intensity of the training went through the roof. I was late twenties and when I was younger the senior pros didn't need to do the running at the end of sessions, but with Strachan we did, we needed to show the younger lads how it was done. Now don't get me wrong, I moaned about it but looking back now that's what gave me an extra year or two at the top flight. The training he did was horrendous but we went into games and we knew the last ten minutes we were still fit. I was the fittest I had ever been under him because of how he made us train. He also knew how to manage us as a group of senior pros, he never had to have a go at the younger players because he knew we would be doing it for him. The standards he set for us were set so if we didn't meet them we were all punished, so it meant that as players we self-managed so we didn't slip.

He was ruthless, but he was fair. I was on a one year contract and if I played twenty games I got a new deal, which I thought was fair. So you can imagine pre-season I'm flying I want to be fit and flying to get my twenty games. When I got to nineteen I would go knock on his door, **'Gaffer I'm on nineteen, that new contract?'** to which he would reply **'One more game!'** but when I got to twenty there it was, the new contract. He was clever because he didn't just hand you a contract so you could sit back relax knowing you would get an extension, you had to work for it."

## DODD RETURNS

"After my time as a player finished at the club I finished up my career at Plymouth Brighton and Eastleigh. It was great to come back as a coach, because the club was such a big part of my life for such a long time. It was an amazing learning process for me getting to work with George Burley, Alan Pardew, Nigel Pearson and then with John Gorman when we were caretaker manager together for a short spell. I was a sponge at that time so was always learning, I wanted to get all my badges done and be on that training pitch.

I would watch sessions picking out the things I liked and then added those bits with my ideas. Of course then I was also with the academy for five years which was a brilliant."

## COACHING THE NEXT GENERATION

"When I went into coaching, the life skills that Dave Merrington had taught me as a young player had a massive effect on me as a coach. I wanted to have that same impact on the players I was working with. So I would make sure they all had little jobs to do and standards were boots always had to be clean. Obviously it wasn't as strict as it was in my day, but I remember Luke Shaw was in the first team and was trying to get out of the door and I was like **'Where are you going? Get back in here you have jobs to do!'** It was all about that grounding that the players I started my career with still talk about it now.

I worked with some wonderful players like James Ward-Prowse, Luke Shaw and Calum Chambers but for me as a coach it was also about the other players who were really good but not up to the Premier League level. I had a lot of empathy for those players because even though they might not make it at Southampton, I wanted to help them get football elsewhere. I would make phone calls and do work for those players to hopefully get them a career in the game and again that was something I learned from Dave. When players were released he would help get them in to other clubs and clubs would be lining up for them because they knew Dave created not only great players but great lads."

## THE FANS

"When I played we used to be out and about and in and around town all the time. Playing golf, going shopping, we used to be around the fans all the time. You would get fans that came up to you and say well done, but you also got the fans who wanted to have a go. I always used to have a discussion with them and explain them we were doing our best and we were working hard and you hoped they went away understanding where the team was at.

Our supporters, as long as they saw you were running around giving it your all, would have you as a player and support you end of story. I was always open and honest with the fans and I would do, and always still do, what I can do what I can to give back and support the club and fans even now. An hour of my time is nothing, the fans put their heart and soul into the club so why can't I."

# LIFE OF A SAINT

# DAVID PRUTTON

2003 - 2007
**POSITION** : Midfield
**APPS** : 75
**GOALS:** 5

**DEBUT:** 08/02/2003 v Blackburn Rovers

David Prutton signed for Southampton in the January of 2003 from Nottingham Forest. He would be part of the side which finished strongly in 2003 although he was cup tied for the FA Cup Final. Prutton was part of the squad that was relegated to the Championship in 2005, having missed ten games via a suspension after being charged by the FA for the events following his red card for a tackle on Robert Pires. He would make eighty two appearances for the Saints before moving back to Nottingham Forest in January 2007. His career would take him on to Leeds, Colchester, Swindon, Sheffield Wednesday, Scunthorpe and Coventry before hanging up his boots. Since then David has established himself as the main anchor for Championship football on Sky Sports.

**NOTTINGHAM TO THE SAINTS**

"I was very much enjoying myself with a very good team at Forest. I had been offered a new contract which was being suggested I should sign. My agent at the time was very well connected in the game and understood that Southampton could well be a team that was interested in signing me. When you realise a Premier League club wants to come for you, you have to give it some serious thought.

I was very happy, very comfortable and highly motivated at Forest. We had a team that had a good mixture of up and coming players, Paul Hart had brought us all through and believed we could all achieve something if we stuck together, but the more

I thought about it, the more I realised that chances to play in the Premier League may be few and far between. When it became more concrete that a move was on the cards it was something I actively went after with my agent and it came to fruition very late on in that January transfer window.

Gordon Strachan was the Manager at the time and he was a huge factor in the move. I understood his reputation having watched him as a player. Meeting him face to face he was very straight forward, had a wicked sense of humour, very sharp and his assistants Garry Pendrey and Dennis Rofe made an instant impression and proved to be nice foils for what he was like as a Manager.

I knew the club was a long way away from home and I remember driving down the night before to London, being stuck on the motorway because the weather was so horrendous in the middle of the night. The next day me and my agent drove down the M3 to the club and it was a glorious sunny winters day. The stadium was fantastic and having seen the training ground it was somewhere I was looking forward to playing."

## MEETING THE TEAM

"I remember the whole team just being really nice fellas, I got on really well with Paul Telfer and Paul Williams who, of course, had played with Gordon Strachan before. They were a great group and unforgiving when it came to training. People like Chris Marsden set the standards; God forbid your first touch wasn't the right one, as he would be straight on you. It was such a good way of making sure you were up to your best every single day.

Coming into that side having been at Forest where I had been part of the furniture for a while as a younger player, I'm not saying you relax but you knew your place in that dressing room. When you move you have to establish yourself in a new environment.

Jason Dodd was a player I got on with well and James Beattie was the life and soul of the dressing room. He was very outgoing and that personality you saw on the pitch was amplified in the dressing room. Marian Pahars; he was very quiet spoken but was a phenomenal footballer. Fabrice Fernandes - he blew with the wind, one minuet he would look at you like he had never seen you before and the next minute he would be nice as pie.

Claus and the Scandinavian players were as closest to adopted Brits I have ever come across in football. They embraced the English rituals of working hard and playing hard together. It was a very well balanced dressing room with a group of older pros that Gordon Strachan could really depend on."

## 2003 CUP TIED FOR THE FINAL

"I was cup tied for the FA Cup and to be honest that's most probably why the club got there because I couldn't mess it up.

When I moved I knew it was the case because when I was at Forest we had played West Ham, I was Captain in that game and we got knocked out. But it didn't really cross my mind that I wasn't going to be involved. I remember watching Matt Oakley score a couple against Millwall in the fourth round replay, then watching the Semi-Final v Watford.

There was a lot of attention on the club around the final and I remember walking onto the pitch at Cardiff with the rest of the lads and Steve Wigley, who was on the coaching staff said '**This must be pretty tough for you?**' as we stood and took in the atmosphere at the Millennium Stadium. I had never thought about it before, it was one of those things as a footballer you compartmentalised. I knew I was never going to play in it so I didn't really think about it.

The sense of occasion of it all though really got to you when you watched the game. The volume of fans inside the ground was incredible and seeing it up close and seeing how great the fans were is a memory that really will last for me."

## STRACHAN'S DEPARTURE

"From my point of view the minute Gordon Strachan left to spend more time with his family, which we understood, the sense of what he brought to that Southampton team disappeared which was a real shame. Through various states of squad we managed to let things slip."

## PRUTTON SEES RED

"I was talking about this the other week with someone at work when we had Stuart Pearce on Sky Sports. He was the text book hard man and I think he only got sent off once or twice and I looked at my stats and I had been sent off twelve times. So that doesn't make me twelve times harder than Stuart Pearce, it makes me twelve times more stupid than him!

With that red card, I think it was because we were struggling. It was something everyone was talking about, everywhere you went in the city the only topic of conversation was about the situation we were in as a team. Whenever you spoke to fans it was about the relegation battle and knowing how well the club had done year on year at The Dell to stay up, it added to the pressure. With players like Francis Benali, Jason Dodd, and Matt Le Tissier in those sides it meant that when they were in trouble they could pull themselves out of it. I think we lacked the character of those sides of the past to see us through and maybe that was exemplified by me going a bit crazy in a game where we were doing very well.

It was one of the defining moments of my career and on that day I was super pumped up, far too pumped up. I was a player who didn't play on the edge but I threw myself around with gusto to make up for any lack of talent because the Premier League was a tough, unforgiving place and even more so now.

I remember before it and I remember the aftermath. It was just a total red mist and it's something that came to define that season because it reflected how out of control we were as a side.

I was suspended for ten games and fundamentally as a footballer that can't play football on a Saturday you are pretty useless. I had to maintain an upbeat outward persona around the team and around the club during that run in, but not being able to have any tangible effect on a game was frustrating, but I had to get on with it as it was my fault."

## RELEGATION FROM THE PREMIER LEAGUE

"There were glimmers of hope with some of the performances from the likes of Peter Crouch, Jamie Redknapp and Graeme Le Saux, but ultimately the club got relegated and succumbed to that killer blow and we went down. There was a lot of change after that, players moved on, coaching staff changed. Harry Redknapp stuck around for a little bit but it was a difficult time.

I remember talking to Graeme Le Saux not too long ago and we were speaking about it all and I forgot that was his career finished at the end of that season. So in the sense it was interesting as to what that season also meant for a player like Grahame and also Jamie Redknapp, because that relegation was the end to their careers. For me, I went on and carried on playing but for them it was a full stop to what had been, up to that point, two illustrious careers."

## HARRY REDKNAPP

"He was great fun, he was a lively presence. He left a lot of the coaching to Kevin Bond and Jim Smith. He obviously didn't get the warmest of welcomes and even Harry admitted crossing that divide is something he wouldn't do again. The hatred that exists between Southampton and Portsmouth is as white hot as I have seen in a football rivalry. I remember when I went to the FA to get hauled across the coals and get my wrists slapped he was there with me. It was a unique experience to have Harry on one side and my PFA representative on the other trying to defend me as we listened to the long list of disciplinary complaints. I basically didn't have a leg to stand on."

## LIFE IN THE CHAMPIONSHIP

"For me, it was back to a level of football I had known for a long time, having played Premier League football, which was something I had always dreamt of, you could say it was back to earth with a bump. I thought we had a good enough set of players to bounce back, but I knew that any side that had come down from the Premier League would be a team other sides would raise their game against. It was imperative that we banished the shadow of the relegation quickly.

It certainly wasn't as straight forward as we first thought it would be, it was a side in the state of flux which didn't help, we knew it was going to be a battle and keeping the best players in that squad was so important and there were a fair few ins and outs which didn't help. Premier League football just seems to suit a club like Southampton. They always had

Managers that wanted to play football in a certain way that was pleasing on the eye, but at that time there was lots of change with managers in an out. It was a bit of a revolving door after Strachan left and it felt like this huge football club was allowed to just meander to where it did over the following years before bouncing back so well."

## JANUARY 2007 PRUTTON RETURNS TO FOREST

"It was a bit of a disaster to be honest but, it was a nice bit of familiarity away from a situation that had become increasingly frustrating.

I had a broken my toe and then I knackered my ankle in that season. The summer before, I had agreed a move to Leeds but failed a medical. I came back to Southampton and under went surgery which, in hindsight, actually added a few more years on to my career, I had had a tough two years at Southampton and I wanted to be somewhere with familiar surroundings. Forest were in League One and looking to get promoted. I went there and there was an assumption from the fans that because I had gone away and played Premier League and Championship football I would take to it like a duck to water, but I found it tough.

I was never a player who was going to come in and score you ten to fifteen goals a season or be the one who would be an instrumental playmaker. Yes you would get effort, yes you would get endeavour and a total commitment to the cause but God bless you if you were looking at me to win you games.

I managed to help the side get into the Play Offs that year, but then completely negated any positive influence I had had by getting sent off in the Semi-Finals. Forest had taken over my contract from Southampton so at the end of the season I went and saw the Manager at Forest Colin Calderwood and he put his arms out and said '**There is nothing I can do for you**'. Obviously going in to try and get a contract after being sent off at a crucial time wasn't the best audition. So that really marked the end of my four and a half years at Southampton that had flown by."

## MY TIME AT THE SAINTS

"From a personal point of view, I made friends in the city, I met my wife in Southampton and all my extended family are from there. My son is a Southampton fan and my father in law actually played for Southampton, he played in the Mick Channon era so he is a proper former Saint. My family down here very much like to take the mick and say '**Remember everyone, David's son, his Grandad used to play for Saints**' and I stand there like a wally saying '**Thanks for that I played for them too you know**'.

I see it as a few years I really enjoyed and look back on fondly. The last few years were tough because of my injuries, but before that I had been very lucky and didn't miss much football. For me being able to say I was a Premier League player, all be it of a certain category or ilk is very special, it's something no one can take away from me and Southampton afforded me that.

It's a beautiful part of the world, the people I met down there were very down to earth. Even going back with my TV work there are so many familiar faces still at the club. It's always great to see everyone like the stewards, they always greet you with a smile and a shake of the hand which I always treasure.

I remember going to a game recently and I was walking up to the gantry and these two ladies were clapping me saying welcome back which was really nice.

The club deserves its place in the Premier League and I'm sad I was part of a team that took them down, but I count myself extremely lucky that they took a punt on me and I count myself lucky to have worn the shirt and to have been a Saint."

# LIFE OF A SAINT

# MIKE EARLS

1970-1975
POSITION : Defender
APPS : 8

DEBUT: 26/02/1974 v Liverpool

Mike Earls joined Southampton as a schoolboy after being scouted in Ireland by Ted Bates. The Irish schoolboy player came to Southampton aged just sixteen. He made his debut away at Anfield v Liverpool in 1974 and although he would only go on to play eight games for the first team, he was a well liked played in the squad at Southampton and after leaving the club he went on to play for Aldershot Town.

### THE BOY FROM LIMERICK BECOMES A SAINT

"As far back as I can remember all I wanted to do was play professional football. I played all sports when I was a kid including Gaelic football, hurling and every game I could really. At fifteen I had to make a decision on what sport I was going to play and I chose football.

I broke into the Irish schoolboys' team which resulted in Ted Bates coming over to Ireland to watch me. I wasn't aware he was coming over on that particular weekend and before I knew it I was being offered an opportunity to come over for a months trial at Southampton.

Apparently at the time there was also interest from Leeds United and Coventry in me. Ultimately it came down to a decision of going to Leeds for trials or Southampton. The scout who was around at the time advised me to go to Southampton and that's what I did.

When I left to go to Southampton it was the first time I had been outside Limerick. I arrived on a Sunday night and it was Ted who picked me up from the railway station in Southampton, although initially I missed the station and ended up in Bournemouth.

On the Monday morning I was taken down to The Dell by Mr Saunders who was the printer of the match day programmes for the club, he owned a lovely B&B off Winn Road where I was staying. I was absolutely amazed just walking into The Dell, all the buzz and seeing all of these famous players who I had only ever seen photographs of back in Ireland.

That morning Ted Bates called me into his office which was quite plush, there was a great big picture of Wembley behind his desk and he sat there and he said '**Right Mike, welcome to the club. You're here for four weeks. I want you to enjoy yourself, I just want you go play and just do what I know you can do. If you have any problems think of me as an Uncle just come and tell me**' and that was just amazing for me.

After that I went off down into the reserve team dressing room to get ready to train. I can remember people like Bill Beaney, Nick Holmes, Pat Earles and Stevie Middleton being in there and then in the home team dressing room were all the big guys. Terry Paine, Ron Davies, John McGrath and Jimmy Gabriel to name a few. I was sixteen at this point and I remember feeling like a fish out of water.

We went up to Wide Lane to do a session and it was firsts v seconds. I was put in at the back for the seconds, I looked up and just saw Terry Paine, Ron Davies, Mick Channon, Brian O'Neil, Hughie Fisher and Dennis Hollywood staring back at me and I can remember clear as day standing there thinking, '**Have I died and gone heaven?**' and that was my introduction to Southampton Football Club.

I did my four weeks and Ted called me in and said '**We want to sign you on as an apprentice professional**'. I flew back to Ireland for Christmas, it had been a tough time as I was very homesick having never been outside Limerick. I remember sitting down with my family and my dad asked me what I wanted to do. Of course I wanted to play football, so I signed the forms and the came back in the January."

### EARLS SETTLES IN
"When I arrived back I was given the club book of rules which laid out what was expected of me and I was given my club blazer with the badge on and it was a phenomenal moment for me and one of real pride. My Southampton adventure was about to begin.

I joined a really good crop of young lads and some of them went on and made the grade. I had to do some catch up because I only had a little bit of experience of playing at an Irish schoolboy level with people like Liam Brady, but those early days were brilliant.

I was put in digs with Ken Jones and Wayne Talkes, we lived with a Mr and Mrs Hart and Percy Hart, who worked in the commercial office at the club. They were all really supportive and really looked after me, helping me settle. I remember before I left Ireland being told that I had to dig in and stay for at least six months, no matter how homesick I felt. It was hard mentally and emotionally but I did it and it all worked out fine.

I played for Southampton A, which was great experience because we played in Hampshire One and that was a very tough league. We would play teams like Newport in the Isle of Wight and the US Navy. We would have some cracking games which was a really good learning curve. We also had a great coach with the A team, a gentleman called Bill Stroud, he was a great character and was very supportive of us as a group of young lads.

Myself, Bill Beaney, Nick Holmes and Stevie Mills made it through our first two or three years and we worked hard to earn our spurs on a day to day basis and we also had to work hard to earn the respect of all those amazing players who were in the first team.

I can recall playing in a reserve match at Ipswich with John McGrath who was coming back from injury. I made a mistake and he literally gave me a dig and said '**You can't do that!**' and that's what it was like. You couldn't make mistakes, if you did you got found out very quickly."

## TRAINING WITH LEGENDS

"We had some fierce matches in training, I was looking to try and get into the team and make my mark. Playing against Mick Channon, Ron Davies and players like that, they didn't take training lightly. They used those matches to hone their skills and their abilities too.

We got to know them quite well in training, we got to know how they played and that was a great privilege to train against. Like Ron Davies who was one of the great headers of the ball, Mick Channon who was an incredible striker and Terry Paine who had an absolutely amazing football brain and he was such a great passer of the ball. To be on that training pitch with them was magnificent. I was also very lucky to get great support from John McGrarth and Tony Byrne.

I remember one day training with Tony. We were passing balls twenty to thirty yards to each other and he was having to work to get them. So in he sidled up to me and said '**Mike you're going to have to do something about these passes, because if you're doing this with Terry Paine he will murder you and let everyone know how rubbish you are at this.**' Tony was a big help that day, because as a young player coming into the game all of a sudden you're having to up your game when you were around the first team. Tony was an international for Ireland and was very well respected, so having him support me at that time was brilliant."

## BREAKING INTO THE FIRST TEAM
"Having been around the first team players and had the experience of playing against them in training was fantastic because I was always watching, listening and learning. I had the opportunity to see how the players behaved every day and particularly before matches.

If you were not playing you were at the ground helping behind the scenes, dealing with the kit, helping the coach or just there to be of assistance. This meant I got to see how these greats professionals got prepared for a game. Players like Mick Channon would come in twenty minutes before, get changed and go out, but players like John McGrath would come back from the pre-match meal and hour and a half before kickoff and start preparing. He would make sure he was well oiled, making sure he had everything he needed before heading to the gymnasium to do a bit of a warm up. For me, getting a feel for that was invaluable especially when it came to walking out in front of 30,000 people at The Dell.

When the time did come for my debut I was ready. Lawrie McMenemy was now the Manager and decided to give myself, Bill Beaney and Nick Holmes a try. I got my opportunity at a game away at Liverpool.

It was amazing, firstly to be thinking that I was going to go and play at Liverpool and secondly to be given my opportunity to step up to show what I could do. Players like Hugh

Fisher were very supportive and as far as they were concerned I was good enough to do the job. Seeing my name on the first team list and that I was going to Liverpool will be something that will never leave me."

## LIVERPOOL v SOUTHAMPTON 26th FEB 1974

"Before we went up, John McGrath gave me some really good encouragement and advice. He said **'Right this is want you are going to do. Take a deep breath before you go out, make sure you know who you're going to be dealing with, get a good tackle in early and make your mark'**.

When we got to Liverpool, Bill Shankly was there watching us arrive and in the dressing room there were a few telegrams that had been sent to me wishing me well. I remember having a real sense of pride as I put on that first team shirt that day. Wearing the Saints first team shirt for the first time you felt six foot six tall, knowing you were about to go out and represent club and the city.

Once the game started though, the only thing on my brain was John's words. So when the opportunity came to make my mark I took it. Playing out wide that day was a player called Peter Cormack and, as we did in those days, we went in to tackle hard, you didn't go in to hurt people, you just made sure they felt your presence. I took him out right in front of that Liverpool dugout with Shankly and his entourage watching on and I felt absolutely brilliant.

I won the ball, cleared it away and I remember running back to get into position thinking **'That's it, I'm settled into this game'**.

I remember enjoying the match and had no nerves at all. I didn't have a single nerve in my body, from the moment I arrived at the ground to when I went out onto the pitch hearing the roar of the crowd. We played well that day and were unlucky to lose 1-0, we had chances to win as well with Mick Channon having three or four great chances.

When the game had ended at Liverpool I wanted more, I loved it, I loved every second. Playing in front of thousands of people in a ground full of history it really was a day I will never forget. When we got back Lawrie McMenemy came up to me and said **'Great debut,** if you play like that you will see the world.' Two years later I was at Aldershot, so I always wonder what went wrong."

## MISSING OUT ON THE NEXT GAME
"Unfortunately after the Liverpool match which we played on a Tuesday night I picked up an injury in training. We had the Wednesday off and we came back in and trained on Thursday morning. In that session I did something to my back, I was only eighteen and had never had back trouble so couldn't explain it. It ruled me out of the game that weekend which was at Highbury against Arsenal, it was really disappointing for me as I wanted to play a few more games at least to show the Manager what I could do.

Nick Holmes made his debut in that game v Arsenal and that was the start of an incredible career for him. For me it was when my downfall began, going from an un-explainable high on the Tuesday full of confidence having achieved my dream, to then to having this injury and things taking a turn in the wrong direction. The injury knocked me back and then other people came in in front of me and I didn't play again until the Easter v West Ham."

## TWO GAMES AT THE DELL - EASTER 1974
"The team was struggling over the Easter period and I was called in to play in firstly v West Ham and then v Manchester United at The Dell. This time I was making my home debut which was very special.

Running out at The Dell was a completely different experience to Liverpool. It was awesome, a full house, probably more than 30,000, the place was heaving. The West Ham side had Trevor Brooking, Frank Lampard Senior and Clyde Best playing for them that day.

There was a lot of pressure on us all at the time and I remember giving away a corner kick at the Archers Road end. Jim Steele came up and he tapped me on the face and he said **'Don't do that again!'** So I said **'Ok Jim'**. I was concentrating on getting organised for the corner and then he did it again, tapped me in the face and said **'Don't do that again!'** My immediate reaction was to turn around and hit him. The next day in the papers there was a photograph of a busy goal mouth and Jim Steele's head going back after I had whacked him.

Lawrie McMenemy put a very good spin on it and said '**It shows my team are fighting, not just each other but also to get results.**' Thankfully Jim never picked it up with me, he caught me at training once but he didn't make a deal about it at the time. I recall us playing well in the game and we could and should have won the match but we drew 1-1. Then on Monday we played Manchester United and again the points were important.

It was a full house and, like us, Manchester United were struggling. Lou Macari and Brian Greenhoff were playing in that game and it was a great experience to go up against them. I loved every second of it and loved playing in front of the Southampton fans at The Dell. It was another draw for us in that match and it again finished 1-1 with Mick Channon scoring our goal."

## EARLS MOVES ON BUT SOUTHAMPTON IS ALWAYS HOME

"We sadly got relegated that season and I played in a few games towards the end, one against Burnley and one against Everton which we won but it wasn't enough to keep us up. We dropped into the second division and I played three games for the first team before I left and went to Aldershot. Southampton has always remained home, ever since I moved from Ireland. For me it sits on a parallel with Limerick. I met my lovely wife Irene here and there is just something about the city that means a lot to me.

My life has always been about the club and it still is. It's in my DNA. I've had the privilege of getting to know so many great people in Southampton particularly through the football side of life. The legends like Cliff Huxford and Bryn Elliott and all the teammates I grew up with; Bill Beaney, Nick Holmes and Steve Mills to name a few. Great footballers but also great people. I love speaking to the fans and having great discussions with them and I still love the excitement of going to see the boys play at St Mary's."

## TED BATES - MY HERO

"Ted Bates was my hero. He changed my life by coming over to Ireland and bringing me to Southampton. His love of the game was infectious and in training if we were playing firsts v seconds he would never let us stop unless first team were winning. You would be out there for ages until he got a result. He dedicated his whole life to Southampton in the various roles that he played. To me he was an outstanding gentleman and he always will be and I love that great statue that we now have outside the ground of him. To have had that experience when he sat me down in that room and said '**You can play football, I've brought you over here so show what you can do**' was incredible.

I remember contacting the club once to see if I could take my father-in-law around to The Dell to show him the club as he was a huge fan, I didn't hear anything back straight away and then I got a call one day from Ted. He said '**Michael I understand you want to bring your father-in-law to the ground to show him around and you would like me to be part of that?**' Now I always called him Boss, I never called him by his first name and I said '**Yes please if that's ok boss?**'

So one morning we went down to the ground, we were pulling into the carpark at The Dell and all of a sudden Ted arrived. He took us on a tour of the ground which was so special for my father-in-law. Ted took us all around and led us out down the steps and out to the pitch. Now I had my camera and said '**Boss is it ok to get a picture of you both on the pitch?**' To which Ted said '**Hang on a minute I need to ask the groundsman first**' and I thought '**That's why Ted is Mr Southampton**'. He could do what he wanted, but he had that respect for everyone and their role that he wouldn't go onto the pitch without the permission of the groundsman.

Without that great man I wouldn't have had the amazing opportunity to play for this great club and for that I am truly thankful and that's why he is my hero."

## EARLS LAST GAME AT 56 FOR THE EX-SAINTS

"I retired from football at the age of fifty six playing my last Ex-Saints match over in Cork where we went for a big charity match for a young girl who had passed away. An Ex-Ireland international had put the game on and the whole of Ireland was involved.

I thought if I'm going to play my last game this is the place it has to be. In a Southampton kit back in Ireland where it all began. So that was my last game and I still have my boots with the mud on from that game in Cork."

## TRIBUTE TO THE FANS

"I want to pay tribute to all Saints fans over the period of my life in Southampton. As a regular supporter and occasional speaker at St Mary's, I admire the loyalty and commitment and stoic determination often against the odds and elements throughout the season to follow the Red and White, truly awesome.

All the players I had the privilege of working and playing with were wonderful professionals who gave their all for the club and played their part in its great history. What we have today at St Mary's was built on the great dedicated people such as Directors of the past, Bowyer and George Reader. Managers like Ted Bates, Lawrie McMenemy. Players including Terry Paine, Nick Holmes, Mick Channon, Peter Osgood, Ron Davies, John McGrath and Jimmy Gabriel.

I had the privilege of playing with and against some outstanding footballers on a daily basis and at some of the great stadiums in England. My career in football continues regardless in some fashion. I think I played with more great footballers in my Ex-Saints period and in the reserves era than in my actual career which was awesome and rewarding in many many ways."

# LIFE OF A SAINT

# DANNY WALLACE

1977 -1989
**POSITION** : Striker
**APPS** : 299
**GOALS:** 79

**DEBUT:** 29/11/1980 v Manchester United

**SAINTS HONOURS** : 1983 - 1984 First Division Runner Up, 1983 - 1984 Goal of the Season

Danny Wallace became a Saint in 1977 aged just thirteen when he joined the youth set up. He turned professional in 1982 but by that time he had already made his debut and was making an impact. His debut came at Old Trafford when he ran out for the first time alongside Rueben Agboola, who also made his first appearance that day. Aged just 16 years and 313 days old, the 29th November 1980 would be the start of an incredible career. Many more unforgettable games were to follow including v Liverpool in the 1983 - 1984 season; a year when Saints would finish runners up in the First Division.

Another memorable night awaited him in 1988 when he was joined by his brothers Rod and Ray in the Saints starting line up at The Dell v Sheffield Wednesday. It was the first time three brothers were playing in the same side in the English top flight since 1920 and all three went on to establish themselves in the side that season. Danny Wallace made 253 appearances for Southampton scoring 64 goals, before he joined Manchester United in 1989.

### DANNY BECOMES A SAINT AT 13 YEARS OLD
"I had a PE teacher at school called Keith Hodder and had read in the paper that Southampton were looking for young players to go to their London academy, although back

then it was called the schoolboys association. So I went down to Slough where I did a bit of training and then I went on to have a trial. There were some amazing players in there like Rueben Agboola and Stevie Baker who were a year or so ahead of me. The majority of us got an apprenticeship with the club and for me from there it all went the right way.

As soon as Southampton told me I was going to be on their books as an apprentice I was really looking forward to it. I grew up in a place called Deptford with my mum and dad and I wanted to get out of London as soon as I could, so I was really looking forward to moving down to Southampton and to be going to do something that I really loved doing which was playing football. It was just fantastic to be joining such a big club like Southampton."

## MANCHESTER UNITED V SOUTHAMPTON - OCTOBER 1989:
## WALLACE MAKES HIS DEBUT AGED 16 YEARS AND 313 DAYS OLD

"I was doing pretty well in the youth team games and played a few reserve matches but I hadn't really done any training with the first team and I didn't know I would be going to United until the day before. I went to Manchester thinking I was going to look after the players and get their boots and kit ready. I never realised I was about to make my debut.

As we got off the coach I was still carrying in all the kit off to the dressing room for the players. I remember going out onto the pitch to have a look and just being overwhelmed at the theatre of dreams, it was an amazing feeling just being there. We came in about quarter to two and the Manager read out the team sheet. He read out my name and said to me **'You're playing, you're going to be wearing Kevin Keagan's number seven shirt and you're making your debut'**. I didn't really have any time to think about it, I can remember not being at all nervous, I just got my kit on and went out for a warm up and that was it. It was unbelievable.

I can't remember any of the game at all. It was just a blur, I remember more of what happened after and my interview with John Motson for the TV. I think I played alright and Lawrie McMenemy made it really easy for me and I was happy to have made my debut that day. Because I only found out just before the game I couldn't tell my mum, dad or brothers that I was playing, I had to do that after the match and when I spoke to my mum after she was delighted for me.

It was a great time to break into the side as we had some great internationals at the club. The likes of Kevin Keegan, Mick Channon, Chris Nicholl, Dave Watson and Alan Ball. To be honest I could reel off the whole team. It was a great squad of players that I looked up to, so for me being able to learn from them was brilliant and they always made me feel so welcome."

## 1983 - 1984 WHAT A SPECIAL SEASON

"We had a lot of senior pros with experience that season, from Peter Shilton to Mick Mills and Steve Williams. The side had a strong combination of experience and youth coming through. It blended together really well, we had a great season and were very unlucky not to get anything out of.

We got to an FA Cup Semi Final v Everton which was played at Highbury. I think we were unlucky we didn't get through to the final; the FA Cup was something I really wanted to win. Growing up as kid I remember watching it on the TV and all I wanted to do was play football so I could get the chance to play at Wembley and win the FA Cup. Unfortunately it wasn't to be our year.

We had fantastic team though and Liverpool were very lucky we didn't catch them in the league because it was very close with just three points in it."

## GOAL OF THE SEASON - BICYCLE KICK v LIVERPOOL

"I have seen it a few times since, Mark Wright laid the ball off to Frank Worthington, who laid it off to Mark Dennis. He hit the far post cross which Mark Wright headed back across for me. I saw an opportunity to turn my back to do the bicycle kick and luckily for me it went in. I think it could have gone anywhere to be honest but that was a special goal and I was pleased it won Goal of the Season too."

## 1988 THREE BROTHERS TAKE TO THE FIELD

"I'm five years older than Rodney and Ray and I was in the team when they arrived so it was good for them coming in as they could come in and do their thing with me already being there.

22 October 1988 v Sheffield Wednesday was an incredible day for the family. Being able to play in the same game with my brothers was a great feeling. I don't think it will be done again and will be something we can take to our graves.

We played a few games after that together and to be on that pitch with brothers alongside me and our family in the stands was remarkable. It must have been fun for the commentators having three Wallaces on the pitch!"

### YOUNG SAINTS MAKING IT ON THE BIG STAGE: LE TISS, SHEARER AND WALLACE

"It was special for me to grow up with them, I knew they were both players that would go on to do really well. Matt was such an amazing skilful quality player, I'm not surprised how well he did for Southampton at all, he was brilliant. Shearer was a brute, he was made to be a number nine and he done well for Southampton, but when he moved to Newcastle that's when he took on the world. It was great to grow up with them both in the Southampton side."

### TOUGHEST OPPONENTS

"I used to love playing against Paul Parker of Queens Park Rangers. He was a pacey player and I had to use all of my skill to get past him. He was a very hard player to play against because of his pace, but I really enjoyed our match ups.

Stuart Pearce was also another, but I think that was because I was scared of him. He didn't worry about going in and taking you out; he was a strong hard footballer and we had some really good battles. Those two were the two players I really liked to have battles with."

### WALLACE ON THE MOVE

"I was at Southampton for nine years and it got to the stage where I thought I had done all I could to try and get silverware for the team. There were some great young players coming through and I felt that I needed to get a new challenge. Luckily for me Sir Alex Ferguson came in for me, paying £1.2 million which was a record for a Southampton player at the time. It was great to go to United, but I didn't really express myself there. First year I won the FA Cup which was very special because as I said as a kid that was the reason I wanted to play football. The second year I won the Cup winners Cup, but it went downhill from there. I enjoyed my time there but it was the start of the multiple sclerosis starting to set in."

## ONCE A SAINT ALWAYS A SAINT: WALLACE RETURNS IN 2020

"Coming back in the 2019/2020 season and being on the pitch at half time at the Manchester United match I couldn't believe the reception. The fans have been fantastic to me over the years and the fact that they still recognise me and to let me know they are thinking about me is incredible.

The warmth I felt from the fans that afternoon was unbelievable. I had my youngest son Thalia with me pitch side and he was crying as the fans were chanting my name.

It was a joy to be there that day and I love the club so much. Hopefully I will be back there very soon."

# LIFE OF A SAINT

# DENIS HOLLYWOOD

1962 - 1972
**POSITION** : Defender
**APPS** : 266
**GOALS:** 4

**DEBUT:** 02/10/1962 v Scunthorpe

**SAINTS HONOURS** : 1965 - 1966 Second Division Runner Up

Denis Hollywood came to Southampton at the age of fifteen and would go on to make 267 appearances for the club. Originally from Govan in Scotland, Hollywood made his debut just before his eighteenth birthday v Scunthorpe in the League Cup. He would be part of the side which achieved promotion to the First Division in 1966 and also played for Scotland at youth level. He retired at the age of twenty seven and then went on to work in the Southampton Docks.

### THE BOY FROM GOVAN BECOMES A SAINT

"I was born in Glasgow and lived in Govan not too far away from Sir Alex Ferguson. I moved to Essex when I was twelve with a friend of my mothers, who I used to call my grandma, she was a lovely lady and really looked after me.

I went to school in Ilford and always wanted to be a footballer growing up. I was training at West Ham and Tottenham at that stage. It was a great experience for me and that led to me playing for Essex Schoolboys. Not long after that I was spotted by a scout called Jimmy Thompson who invited me to come down to Southampton. Jimmy was a good friend of Ted Bates who was the Manager at the time. I was just fifteen back then and I was put up in digs near The Dell with four or five other apprentices. After that I lived with Cliff Huxford in Shirley and I stayed living with him and his wife until I got married when I was nineteen.

When I first came down though it was for a trial game and after that I doubled up the trip as a holiday with a friend of mine from school. My grandmother called me after the trial and said '**Whatever you do, do not saying anything. Southampton is an awful place to live, please do not sign for them**'. When I got back home I broke the news to her that I had signed and she was devastated."

### THE DEBUT
"I made my debut when I was 17. I was a wing half at the time and we played against Scunthorpe in the League Cup. I found out the day before and I travelled up with the side. It was a great experience. I remember it was a midweek game and on the Saturday we were due to play Preston at The Dell and Ted kept in the side for that game too. So I made my league and home debut in the same week.

Playing for the first team was tremendous. One of my ambitions growing up was to make my first team debut when I was seventeen and I had done that. Eventually I moved to play Full Back, Ted asked me as I was very quick and I could tackle so he felt that position suited me, and that's where I played for the rest of my career."

### INTERNATIONAL FOOTBALL
"I played for Scotland under eighteens in the little World Cup which was very nice. We got to the semi-final and we played England. We were a good team and I would say they had the best team and we were the second best in the competition.

The semi-final was played at the old White City Ground in London, and I think they beat us 1-0 but they had a great side. They went on to play Northern Ireland at Wembley and I think they beat them about 5-0 if my memory serves me right.

I was also picked to play for a Rest of Great Britain side to play England youth at Wembley which was a very exciting day and I also played for Scotland under twenty threes as well."

## TED BATES
"Ted was fantastic, I came down when I was fifteen and I got very homesick. It was a couple of months after I had joined and I had gone home for the weekend. When it got to the Monday morning I didn't go back for training.

Ted was coming to watch West Ham play in a midweek game and he came to see me to find out what was going on. I met him at the train station and we got a taxi to my house where he spoke to me and my grandmother about me and my prospects. He really helped settle my worries and gave me lots of reassurance. Afterwards, he took me to the game at West Ham and after the game he took me back to Southampton.

After that, I remember my grandmother used to write to him all the time, she must have driven him mad, saying '**Make sure you look after him he's only fifteen**' and would send him instruction to make sure I was doing all the right things.

He was a wonderful guy and I liked him very much."

## 1966 PROMOTION TO THE FIRST DIVISION
"We went up with Manchester City that year, they were Champions and we were runners-up. It was fabulous being in the First Division, it was a big jump from the Second Division. We came up against some great players and teams. It was a wonderful time and personally for me it was fantastic to be playing at the top level."

## SOUTHAMPTON ON TOUR
"You see all these sides that now go on international tours, but we were doing it a long time ago, we went all over the world. I remember the year we got promotion - we went to Malaysia and Singapore with Leicester City and played them in some exhibition games.

We went to El Salvador and Honduras on tour with Chelsea, which was quite interesting because the year before El Salvador and Honduras went to war over a football match and when we looked at the itinerary they had put the teams in the same hotel.

We had three weeks in Bermuda, the most beautiful place in the world at the time. We were supposed to play Celtic but for some reason they didn't make it out, so we played West Ham instead.

We went to some beautiful places with Southampton, which was brilliant as I got to see some amazing parts of the world while playing the game that I loved."

## TEAMMATES

"Martin Chivers used to live around the corner from me when I lived with Cliff, I liked Martin he was a great lad and a fantastic player. John Sydenham lived next door and I was so lucky to grow up with such a great group of players. Big Ron Davies, Jimmy Gabriel, John McGrath, Jimmy Steele, they were all tremendous players. Brian O'Neil and I still speak to him at least once a week. I was also great friends with Tommy Jenkins; Ted Bates signed him from Reading, he's in America at the moment.

What we had as a team was the will to win and a pride in playing for Southampton. Me and Brian O'Neil were talking once and we said '**It's not down to the Manager, it's down to the players on that pitch and their will to win**', it was a great group of players and I had such a fantastic time being part of it."

## TRIP TO MICK CHANNON'S STABLES

"Brian O'Neil and myself got invited up to Mick's stables a couple of years ago. Driving up we went in Brian's car, he's the most awful driver! It's frightening sitting in the car with him. I offered to drive but he wanted to take his dog and didn't want it to eat the inside of my car. We got up there safe enough and as we pulled in it was a beautiful place. He had these lovely barns and he was hosting an owners day.

There were about 200 people there and we were given champagne as we arrived, all of a sudden Mick came over and said '**You two come with me, I want you to meet someone**', we followed him and it was Jimmy Tarbuck. Jimmy then tapped his glass and said '**Ladies and Gentleman, if I could please have your attention**' to which the whole room went silent, '**I'd like to introduce two of the dirtiest football players I've ever seen in my life**'. The room roared with laughter and it wasn't a bad way to start a really terrific day with Mick at the stables."

## MIKE SUMMERBEE

"Mike used to play for Swindon and he was a big centre forward, he could dish out a bit and he was a big guy. Whenever we played against Swindon, which was a bit of a derby in my day, I used to make sure he didn't have a good day against me like he did against lots of other defenders. He wasn't frightened of anything, nothing fazed him and there was a little bit more contact in those days, so as the games would go on we had a few tussles. He used to walk past me in The Dell before the game and say **'Make sure you've got your shin pads on!'**

He then moved to Manchester City. Joe Mercer signed him in 1965 and they then put him out on the wide right. In 1969 they had reached the FA Cup Final but for the last game of the season the week before they came to The Dell to face us. We passed each other in the corridor before the game and he said **'We will be alright today Den won't we?'** he was obviously preempting not getting injured ahead of the final.

Now he denies this but, I was told this by the players on our bench at the game. He was caught three or four times in the first five minutes of the game, so he went across to the Man City bench and Mike said to Joe Mercer **'Get me off this pitch!'** We won the game 3-0 that day so he certainly kept a low profile."

## HOLLYWOOD RETIRES AT 27

"When I came into the game I was very single minded, all I wanted to do was play growing up and I had achieved that. I had been at the club a long time and Ted Bates phoned me up and said that he wanted to see me. I went in on the Sunday morning, he took me into his office and he said that he was releasing me and he was telling me now because he was putting it in the papers the following day and that was it.

When I was released I went to Blackpool for a month, came home after a week and decided I had had enough. I then went to Bath City for a couple of months and then finished up at Basingstoke with Cliff Huxford, but within three or four months I had packed it all in. I just knew I wasn't going to achieve what I wanted to at that point, so I retired at the age of twenty seven and went to work in the docks."

## WHAT SOUTHAMPTON MEANS TO HOLLYWOOD

"The fans of Southampton are fantastic and I love Southampton. Growing up and being from Glasgow you either supported Celtic or Rangers, I was a Celtic boy even though I loved our oppositions' Rangers ground, but Southampton is the first result I look out for.

Even though I'm quite old now and I'm not that well known, people still stop me and say '**I remember you**' I always say back '**Well you must be older than I am then or a very big Saints fan?**'

I have lived here since 1960, Southampton is my home. I had the most fantastic lifestyle as a footballer; I joined the club when I was fifteen and didn't stop playing until I left the club when I was twenty seven. I played with some great footballers through the years at the Saints. Playing for Southampton was the greatest time in my whole life."

# MANNY ANDRUSZEWSKI

1972 - 1980
POSITION : Defender
APPS : 98
GOALS: 3

DEBUT: 01/02/1975 v West Bromwich Albion

Manny Andruszewski signed as a schoolboy for Southampton in 1970. He would go on to establish himself at the club making 83 appearances. He made his debut v West Bromwich Albion in 1975 and played a notable role in the route to the 1979 League Cup Final, although he didn't feature in the final at Wembley. Having spent eight years at the club he then moved to the United States of America to play for the Tampa Bay Rowdies in search of regular first team football and a brief return to the Saints in 1982 before his career took him to Aldershot, Andover and the Houston Dynamos.

## ANDRUSZEWSKI BECOMES A SAINT

"It was Ted Bates who signed me at the club, I remember having a trial at Wide Lane on a cold wet Sunday. Ted was there and I must have caught his eye.

There was a scout at the club called Tom Parker and after the trial he used to constantly come around to my house to get me to sign schoolboy forms and my mum used to send him away. My parents weren't into football at all really, and they said this guy kept coming around knocking the door.

I signed schoolboy forms and played for Southampton schools, the fascinating thing about that was that we played our games and trained at The Dell. So that was huge for me as a young player, to be a schoolboy and playing youth games at The Dell that was like **'Wow.'**

After signing schoolboy forms my plan was to go to Taunton College to do my O-levels as I was hoping to become a PE teacher. When I left St Georges secondary in the summer to go on to college, Southampton asked me to go training with them pre-season, I had nothing else going on in the summer so I went along.

I really enjoyed it and come the end of the summer the club asked me to sign, I jumped at the chance, much to my parents' horror. They couldn't comprehend having come from Poland that playing football was a career."

## RUNNING THE LINE

"When I first signed, Ron Davies and Terry Paine were there and I always remember that when you were an apprentice and there was a first team game against the reserves you had to run the line.

If you had the first team end and you flagged them offside you would get so much stick from the players. One week when they were playing, one of the players got injured and they said '**Manny, you have to come on**'. I came on and I had to mark Ron Davies and I was like '**Wow, I have to mark him!**' He could score goals for fun, but I just got stuck in and gave it my all.

To play against players like that and as I progressed the likes of Mick Channon, Peter Osgood, Charlie George, Ted McDougall and Steve Williams in training every single day made playing on a Saturday so much easier".

## SIGNING PRO

"When I signed as an apprentice they offered me the chance to sign as a professional straight from school as I had stayed in school an extra year to do my O levels, but I decided at that time it would be a better grounding for me to become an apprentice. I felt it really benefited me from the discipline side of it. You had to do all the cleaning of the changing rooms and be there early to sort the kit for the players and I really enjoyed that.

After the year I signed my first professional contract and I was ecstatic about it. It was my dream growing up to play for Southampton and here I was signing for them.

With my parents being unable to comprehend the idea initially, being a local lad the recognition it gave them was superb. I think that that meant as much to me as it did signing as a professional".

## THE FIRST TEAM DEBUT v WEST BROMWICH ALBION
"I found out on the Thursday I was going to be involved and we travelled up on the Friday before the game. I remember the gaffer calling me into his office and saying '**You're travelling tomorrow and you'll be playing**'. I can remember quite clearly going back into the changing room laying flat out and shaking like a leaf. I was so nervous and I didn't really know what to expect.

We travelled up on the train and the guys liked to play cards. They asked me to join in so I did, we were playing poker and I remember I won all the money. It's fair to say they weren't too pleased, this young lad rocking up and going away with all the winnings and I was like '**This is great!**'

Steve Mills played left back and I played right back. We won 3-0 and it was an absolutely superb way to start my first team career. I remember in the paper they used to score you out of ten and I got a nine for my debut so I must have played alright.

The next day I had to go into the ground because I picked up an injury and in those days I didn't have a car. I was waiting for the bus and I missed it by two minutes. This guy came past and said '**You just missed the bus, where you going?**' So I told him I was heading to The Dell and he offered me a lift. I introduced myself and he couldn't believe that I had played the night before and I was now in his car."

## THE ARRIVAL OF RODRIGUES
"Lawrie brought in some really good experienced players to the club. Peter Rodrigues was one of them and he became available and came in at right back not long after I had started to come in to the side. So that sort of halted my progression slightly, part of the problem was that I could also play sweeper, centre back, right back or do man for man marking. My main position was right back, but I never really had one position so I could drop in here or

there quite easily which made me quite a useful player to have on the bench. That really hampered my career at the club and I was unable to nail down a regular first team spot".

### 1977 EUROPEAN CUP QUARTER FINALS v ANDERLECHT

"The first leg was in Anderlecht and I had to mark Robert Rensenbrink that night, he was a very well established Dutch International. I remember having a good game and for the return leg the Daily Echo had done an interview with him and asked him '**Who was the most notable player for Southampton from the first leg?**' And he said '**The young guy who has the difficult to pronounce name**', which was me. So I thought he was either trying to soften me up for the return leg or that' was a great compliment coming from a player of his stature. Sadly we lost the tie over the two legs and I got injured in the game at The Dell.

That night after the game Alan Ball offered to give me a lift home. When we got to mine I thought I would invite him in and introduce him to my dad. Now my dad wasn't into football at all and Alan said '**Good evening Mr Andruszewski**' and my dad looked at him and said '**Hello**' followed by '**So do you play football as well?**' Bally didn't know what to say and the look on his face was brilliant. A World Cup winner in our lounge and my dad had no idea who he was."

### THE DELL ON A EUROPEAN NIGHT

"People often ask me what was my favourite ground to play at and for me it was The Dell. It really was the best of them all. Everyone was in such close proximity of the pitch that it created its own very special atmosphere.

The European Games were something different because people were seeing the players that came over from other countries for the first time. It gave the game an extra edge, you were seeing a different type of football and I think the supporters enjoyed that. It just created a real buzz that was very special and unforgettable."

### 3 SPECTACULAR GOALS FOR ANDRUSZEWSKI

"I didn't score many goals but when I did they weren't too bad, there was three in total. The goal v Charlton was pretty special. I played the ball into Mick Channon on the edge of their box, he laid it back to me, I just hit it and it flew into the bottom corner. Funny enough there was a guy who played for Charlton that day, Keith Peacock, and he became the coach when I went to America and I always used to give him some stick about that goal.

There was another goal against Norwich at their place. I started the move just outside of our penalty box. I played it in to Phil Boyer who played it back to me. I then passed it on to Nick Holmes and I started running. He slipped the ball through to me and I hit it with my left foot from just inside the box. I keep watching that one on YouTube, it was pretty special.

And finally my third was against Oldham. It was a wet miserable day and again it was with my left foot outside of the box and the reason why I remember that one was because in one of the papers someone likened me to Sir Alf Ramsey, so I cut that out and made sure I kept it.

There was a couple of own goals thrown in too. One game I was playing against Leicester for the reserves and I put two in my own net and one in theirs, I'm not quite sure if that classifies as a hat-trick or not but it wouldn't be a hat-trick you want!"

## 1979 THE LEAGUE CUP

"I was in and out of the team that season but we were playing Birmingham in the second round and I was picked. Trevor Francis was scoring goals just for fun and so the gaffer said **'I'm bringing you in, I want you to take Trevor Francis out of the game'**. So we walked out on a pitch where he was warming up. I ambled over to him and I said **'Excuse me Trevor, the gaffer has asked me to take you out of the game, but I'm not quite sure if he meant just tonight or permanently?'** and he looked at me not quite sure as to what had just happened. I did my bit and we went on to win 5-2 and I remember travelling back with Ted McDougall. I had been trying to get away from the club because being in and out a team I wanted to play regularly, Ted said **'You have just put another £50,000 on your price tag with a performance like that.'**

We played Leeds in the Semi Final and came in for that game too. I marked Tony Curry and we drew at their place 2-2 and then won 1-0 at The Dell. Charlie George was at the club then and we came in after the game and he came and sat next to me: '**The way you took Tony Curry out of the game won us the tie. That's what got us to the final**'. I remember thinking '**That will be my final because I won't play at Wembley.**' It was great to play that game and help get us to Wembley but it's also one of the biggest disappointments of my career, as I didn't play in that final.

At that time there was only one sub. Myself, Graham Baker and Trevor Hebberd had all featured in several of the games in the route to the final so we thought one of us might get the spot. Instead, Lawrie brought in Tony Sealy who'd played a couple of games for the first team. I was really disappointed because to play at Wembley for Southampton would have been something very special. Lawrie said to us that we were all young enough and we would get another opportunity, but at the time that's not what you wanted to hear."

## MANNY MOVES STATESIDE

"In the summer of 1979 I went to the USA to play for Tampa. There were great players there and it's where I took on Johan Cruyff. He was probably the best player I've ever played against. He was playing for the Washington Diplomats and the Manager said '**I need you to mark Johan.**'

I always remember Alan Ball saying to me '**When you're doing man for man marking you have to make a decision. Some players will try and draw you into positions, that is when you have to decide when to go and when to stay.**' So that was what was in my mind that day.

I was marking Johan Cruyff and he went back into his own half. So I went with him a little bit. Then he went back a little bit deeper and I thought, '**No I will let him go there. He's not causing any problems.**' Then of course he gets the ball, puts on a sixpence, every pass was so incisive. So I thought '**Nope, I need to go a bit tighter even when he's back in his half.**' I followed him and of course that created space. He did this little shimmy, tied me up in knots, hit a sixty yard pass through to his striker who went in and scored, meaning we lost the game 1-0. He was sublime and he was the only player I marked man for man that I couldn't conquer."

## A BRIEF RETURN IN 82

"I had a few medical problems when I was in the United States and I needed to get myself fit. Luckily, Lawrie said I could come back to Southampton to train and see what I could do.

I was fortunate enough that Kevin Keegan was also at that club at the time and I got to do some sessions with him. His work ethic was incredible for a player of his stature. I could see why he achieved what he did because he worked extremely hard. He was always doing extra and at times I was lucky to train with just him.

Sadly it didn't work out and I didn't make any further appearances for the Saints."

## WHAT THE SAINTS FANS MEAN TO ME

"I think being a local I could relate to the fans, just going in ordinary bars and just talking to them. When they used to then watch you play on a Saturday I felt they had some sort of connection to me and I felt they were part of the team as well.

When I finished playing I used to go and watch the Saints quite a lot and you would see the same core of supporters week in week out. It made me really understand that that was what the fans lived for, what they went to work for to go and follow the team. Sometimes as a player you don't realise how much it means, so that's why for me it was so important that I gave my time to the fans and the club.

I remember the fans waiting after games outside and they couldn't pronounce my name, but there was always so much warmth towards me. If you ever did presentations there was always a warm welcome that greeted you which I will always remember and I'm very thankful for."

# LIFE OF A SAINT

# BILL BEANEY

1969 - 1975
POSITION : Defender
APPS : 3
DEBUT: 20/04/1973 v West Ham United

William Beaney signed as an apprentice at the club before signing his professional contract in 1972. Part of Lawrie McMenemy's squad for two seasons, Bill played in both the First and Second Divisions and even featured in Ted Bates Testimonial. In 1975 Bill was released and for his next move he headed off to the United States of America to play for the Washington Diplomats, a move which would lead to an encounter with Pelé.

On his return from the USA Bill came back to the club. This time working on the players entrance and he was a familiar face on match days both at The Dell and St Mary's Stadium.

**BECOMING A SAINT**
"I remember walking past the Manor pub at Netlety and a bloke called Dave Ray came out and said to me '**Where are you going?**' and I said '**I'm going to the Southampton Boys under 11 trails.**' He said '**You won't get in there.**' I said to him that day '**I bet you a shilling I get in the Saints first team**'.

Growing up I used to play for the Manor pub and I also played at all the levels of the Southampton and Hampshire Schoolboys. John Hollowbread (who played for Spurs and was the landlord of the pub) got Bill Stroud (who managed the Saints A side) and Tom Parker to come and watch me play. They saw something in me and I signed Schoolboy forms when I was thirteen which meant I couldn't sign for another club. When I was still at school Saints had four teams, you had the Firsts, the Seconds, the A side and the B side. Most of the B side were amateur and they trained on a Tuesday and Thursday night which I used to go along to.

When I left school at fifteen I signed apprentice forms with the club. Ted Bates and Tom Parker the chief scout signed me for three years until I was eighteen and then when I got to eighteen I signed a three year professional contract.

Growing up I had the offer to go for trials for other clubs, I couldn't have gone because I had signed the schoolboy forms but I wouldn't have gone anyway, Southampton was my team. I remember signing on as an apprentice I was just overwhelmed to be in a room with Tom Parker and Ted Bates. My dad was with me and I was just full of excitement and for me it was like Christmas when you're a kid, it was unbelievable.

I always wanted to play for Saints from when I was ten years old and there I was signing pro, after working my way up the ranks. I had done it."

## BEANEY IN DREAMLAND

"When I was a kid I had scrapbooks I put together dating back to the 1950's right up to when I signed. I used to go get them all signed by the players and, in fact, I still have them all now. So when I turned up to training with all these players I had idolised growing up I was in dreamland. Players like Ron Davies, John McGrath, Jimmy Gabriel and Freddie Kemp. For me, Jimmy Gabriel and Freddie Kemp were my star players, my heroes. When I was an apprentice we had to clean their boots and get all their kit ready, so for me being a fan as well as a player I really was in awe of it all, these were all my heroes."

## BEANEY ON THE TEAM SHEET

"On a Friday at about eleven o'clock they would bring in the team sheets for the weekend and pin them up on the notice board. Now, I never used to look at the first team, I would always just look for my name. On this particular day I looked at the reserve team list and I thought I had been dropped, I couldn't see my name. Now we were on a winning run with the reserves so I couldn't work it out. I looked on the A teams team sheet and I thought **'I'm not even on there? What's going on?'** So I went and sat down and didn't even bother looking anymore and then everyone came over and started saying **'Congratulations Bill you are sub tomorrow at Tottenham for the first team'**.

Saints never really did that well at Tottenham, so as sub I was thinking **'I'm on £25 a week, if I can get on I get £25 appearance money too.'** We were losing with twenty minutes to go and Ted Bates sent me to get warmed up. I thought **'Here we go I'm going to get on.'** I started running up and down getting warmed up and all of a sudden Mick Channon ran through and made it 1-1. I'm jumping up celebrating and then Ted Bates looked at me and said **'Sit down son, you're not going on now.'** So I didn't get my debut or the appearance fee but Mick Channon did go on and score a winner and I was chuffed about it as we had beaten Tottenham.

In the dressing room after all the players had left, I was packing up with George Horsfall and Ted Bates and in came the Chairman George Reader and said **'Ted, who's that nipper who was sub today?'** And Ted went **'Bill Beaney, he's a great lad.'** To which George replied **'Get him sub next week, he's our lucky charm.'** So after that endorsement I was sub the week after at West Ham and the Chelsea."

## WEST HAM v SOUTHAMPTON : BEANEY MAKES HIS DEBUT

"It was Easter Friday and after sixteen minutes Saints were losing 2-0. Jim Steele got injured and Ted looked at me and said **'You're going on!'** This was it, I was about to make my first appearance for the Saints away at West Ham playing against players like Bobby Moore, Trevor Brooking, Frank Lampard Senior, Ted MacDougall, Clyde Best and Billy Bonds.

All I remember thinking was that I was about to play against the World Cup winning Captain Bobby Moore and play with Southampton's very own World Cup winner Terry Paine, it was a pretty special moment.

We lost the game 4-3 and the next day we were due to play Chelsea at Stamford Bridge. I picked up a dead leg in the game and remember going back to the hotel and sitting in the bath with a towel over my thigh all night, putting hot and cold water on it as I didn't want to miss my chance of playing the next day and making my full debut. I did everything I could to get make sure I was fit enough.

Myself and Steve Mills made our full debuts on that day v Chelsea. The team had a few injuries from the day before so that meant we got our chance. The game v Chelsea was incredible, it went so quick, it was an unbelievable day. My ambition was to play for the Saints first team and I had done it. If I never played again I thought to myself '**I had done it!**'"

## 1973 - 1974

"In the 73-74 season I hardly played at all. Lawrie McMenemy arrived at the club and he hardly saw me play, he sent me out on loan to Reading for a month, I came back and then went to Waterford for three months. When I returned at the end of that season Southampton had just been relegated. Lawrie hadn't seen me play as I had either been on loan or injured and I didn't play many games for the reserves.

So he called me into his office and said '**I have spoken to Ted Bates about you and he said you are a good player. So I'm going to give you another years contract, but I need to see more, I'm going to give you another chance.**'"

## THE FINAL SEASON

"The first game in the Second Division was against Hull City and Lawrie started me. We drew 3-3 and that was my home debut. I was disappointed that we didn't win but I now had three games under my belt so was thinking this season I could get myself back in and around the first team. Next up we had Leyton Orient, West Ham and Norwich. I travelled with the side but Jim Steele was fit again and he came back into the side.

After that, Lawrie sent me out on loan again and at the end of that season he gave me a free transfer. My time as a player was over at Southampton, I was obviously disappointed to leave but I was happy to have played for the Saints".

## BEANEY HEADS STATESIDE

"I went to the United States on tour with Waterford who I had previously been on loan with. We were out there for four weeks and we played a few games in New York. At one of the matches, watching on the sidelines was Dennis Viollet who played for Manchester United and was one of the Busby Babes. He was Manager of the Washington Diplomats and asked me if I wanted to sign for them. I jumped at the chance and played for one season. I played every game and it was brilliant, I really enjoyed it."

## WHEN A SAINT PLAYED PELÉ

"When I got released by Southampton there were thirteen of us that all got let go of at the same time, and on the back of the Echo it had picture of all of us with the headline '**The Unlucky Thirteen'**. Some of us were free transfers and some of them were transfer listed.

When I was in America I called my dad and told him that in my second game I would be playing against New York Cosmos and again the great Pelé. It then came to the attention of the Echo and there was a picture of me and a story about me having been part of the unlucky thirteen but was now about to take on Pelé. I couldn't believe it, I was going to play against Pelé. Only a few months before I didn't have a club, I had no job and here I was taking on another World Cup Winner.

He scored two goals in that game and set up another two. He was playing on the opposite side to me, so although I have pictures of us playing I never really got that close to him. He was thirty four at the time and was so sharp and relaxed on the ball.

When we came off the pitch at full time, my dad had sent over the cutting from the paper so I went up to their dressing room and got him to sign it for me. It was a day I certainly won't forget."

## BEANEY RETURNS - THE GATEKEEPER TO THE DRESSING ROOM

"When I came back from America I got a job in Vospers and I was still playing for Poole Town and then Dorchester. In 1990 I stopped playing football and a couple of guys came into my local all dressed up and I said '**Where have you been?**' and they told me they were chief stewards at The Dell and I should give the club a call if I fancied doing it. I applied, and being an ex player I got invited to the first game of the season. Initially I worked on the carpark at Spring Hill School. I would lock the gates at three o'clock and then watch the game stood in the tunnel. I did that for a year and then the guy who did the players entrance couldn't do it anymore. So Barry Fox who was the Assistant Secretary said '**Would you like to do the players entrance?**' And I said to him that I would cut my right arm off to do that, and that was how it all started.

While I was doing it I felt like I was a player again, all the current players became my mates and I used to socialise with them after the games. I got to know the players and staff from the visiting sides and I used to also have all the players tickets so I would see so many former players on a match day. It really was like being part of the team again, only this time without all the training. I did it for seventeen years and loved every minute. Those last games just flew by and it was only a few years later when you look back you realise what you did there and that it was all gone."

"And if you are wondering, Dave Ray never did give me that shilling!"

# JAMES BEATTIE

**1998 - 2005**
**POSITION** : Striker
**APPS** : 188
**GOALS:** 76

**DEBUT:** 16/08/1998 v Liverpool

**SAINTS HONOURS** : 2003 FA Cup Final Runner Up, 98-99 / 02-03 Player of the Year

James Beattie signed for Southampton in July 1998. In his first season he was crowned Player of the Year an accolade he would go on to win a further two times in his time at the Saints. In his eight years at the club he would play a vital role in not only securing survival, but also helping the team to reach the 2003 FA Cup Final v Arsenal at Cardiff.

A prolific goal scorer, the 2002 - 2003 season saw him rack up twenty three league goals which made him the highest English scorer in the Premier League. During his time on the South Coast he also made his England debut v Australia. Beattie found the back of the net sixty eight times in his time with the club before he left to join Everton in January 2005.

### THE SWIMMER BECOMES A FOOTBALLER

"I started swimming when I was about seven and showed a natural talent for it. I trained really hard and when I was thirteen I got scouted by a Great Britain coach that used to coach the Wigan Wasps. Wigan was about forty five minutes from Blackburn where I lived and I would go there in the morning at about 5am to train for two hours. I would then come home, catch the school bus and then go to school. Once I had finished school my mum or dad would pick me up and I would go to training again for another two hours.

Sometimes in the morning I would be the only one who was training in the pool and my mindset was to always try and beat the clock. I would aim for either a national age qualifying time or a record. I think that the resilience I built up trying to beat the clock when I was younger really helped when I moved into football. My dad was a truck driver and he used to work every hour that God sent to try and give us the best of whatever he could and that really helped me growing up, so I wanted to be the best I could. The swimming was brilliant for me and I think a couple of my records still stand now.

Ironically, my aim when I was younger though was not to be a professional footballer or Olympic swimmer. I was very focused on my schoolwork and I wanted to do well in my GCSEs and then my A-Levels because I wanted to go to medical school.

When I was 15 I finished swimming because of a shoulder injury and I started playing more football. I was playing in one game and a guy called, Derek Langley who was a scout for Blackburn, was watching and invited me to go and train with the youth team.

I went along and Dave Jones, who would go on to sign me at Southampton, his son was also training in the same sessions. I was quite a physical player and that's when Dave first noticed me as a player.

After a while at Blackburn I got offered a YTS contract. I then had a decision to make, as I still wanted to go down the academic route at this stage, but here it was - an opportunity to forge a career in football. Now the failure rate is 99.9% in football and I had to weigh it up with my education which dad had worked so hard to support me in.

It was a massive decision because I didn't want to upset my dad by saying **'You know after all that support you have given me and helped fund my education, I now want to be a footballer.'**

My dad was very supportive and he went to the club and ended up negotiating with them to get a one year YTS and two year pro from the off. He came back to me and said **'What do you want to do, this is what they're offering?'**

I remember long discussions with my dad and he said **'At the end of the day it's up to you, but you could go and give this a go, see what happens and you can always fall back on your education. In football this opportunity might never come again'.**

So I had a good think about it and signed for Blackburn Rovers."

## BLACKBURN TO SOUTHAMPTON
"Roll on five years in my development, I was now twenty and was doing well at Blackburn. I made my debut at eighteen against Arsenal in the Premier League and had made a few more subsequent appearances after that for the first team. I had just had a really good season in the Reserves but Kevin Davis had just signed from Southampton and that made me available for a move.

At this point I believe Dave Jones rang Stuart Ripley, who had joined Saints, to ask about me, having seen me play at an earlier age. **'What's he like? Should we get him?'** and Stuart said **'Yes'**.

I got a phone call from the secretary saying that Southampton would like to speak to me. I went down, but I was quite apprehensive as I'd lived at home for twenty years, this would be a big lifestyle change for me.

I met Dave Jones at Enio's at the bottom of the town. He explained what he was doing at Saints, what he wanted from me and he was brilliant. It all felt right, Dave was a good Manager and I signed in the summer of 1998."

## THE DEBUT v LIVERPOOL AT THE DELL
"I used to love The Dell, but I didn't realise at that time what a significant part it would play in my development and career and the good times we would have there. So making my debut at The Dell was brilliant but I can't really remember much about the game.

I came on as a sub and knowing what I was like I would have wanted to have been starting, but I understood that I was going into a well-established traditional club with some great players in the dressing room. Le Tissier was one of them and there were other players like Egil Østenstad. I knew I had my work cut out to try and get a starting place in the team.

I settled in really quickly and remember Stuart Gray and Dennis Rofe who were coaches at the club being brilliant for me when I joined. It was a great dressing room to be part of and very welcoming."

## THE DRESSING ROOM
"When I joined, Gary Monk was one of the younger players in and around the first team squad and we became friends straight away. Obviously in my coaching career I've worked with him for seven years now, but that friendship started in my early days at Southampton when we used to spend a lot of time together.

The dressing room was brilliant, we had players like Matt Le Tissier and Franny Benali in there. Dave Hughes, Matt Oakley, Richard Dryden and Claus Lundekvam were all just really good lads. Having then been in the dressing room for a few months, I could see how they'd manage to keep their Premier League status, there was a real togetherness that they had that you really felt part of.

We were never a team of real stars, maybe apart from Le Tissier but the team spirit and the camaraderie mixed with that togetherness is what got us through the difficult times and also the successful times we had too."

## PLAYER OF THE SEASON 98-99
"I knew I had my work cut out to establish myself in the team, with my previous experiences with swimming and my upbringing, I was determined to do it and I had a lot of resilience. I worked until November to try and get myself into the side and to try and get a run of games.

I remember speaking to the Manager about it and he gave me my chance in the November and I didn't look back. It was obviously an honour to win Player of the Year that season which was a great great achievement for myself, but the overriding factor for me was that I was able to help the club survive avoiding relegation in the great escape year.

A few games that really stood out for me that season was the Blackburn 3-3 and then the Everton 2-0 game where Marian Pahars scored two."

## DEALING WITH INJURY AND BARON SPELLS IN FRONT OF GOAL
"I've always had an unbelievable self-belief, and it's something that I pass on to the players that I coach now. I understand that the landscape has now changed with regards to social

media and people having their say about you, but I think if you believe in yourself and never let that belief waver you can get through the tough times like when I wasn't scoring or had an injury.

In training I would go back to the things that I was good at, such as the process of getting myself ready for a game on a Saturday and trying to rekindle feelings that I had when I was on those good scoring runs. I was always massively self-confident and a lot of people might take that for arrogance but if you are self-confident it's just a mindset thing for me.

Throw all those things into the mix with what I learnt from swimming, my upbringing and memories of when I had tough times as a youngster or got beaten in a swimming gala, it all helped. The only thing to do then was to work hard, get back in the pool or on the pitch, get better, keep trying, and that's exactly what I did."

## 23 LEAGUE GOALS 2002 - 2003

"The team was developing really well at that point and I was growing as a player. I think one of the main reasons for my goal tally was the fitness level of the team. We were so fit we could just keep going till the end and there was always a collective effort from everybody, I just happened to be the one getting the goals. I would come in after games and feel that I could actually play another game because we were that physically fit.

Our mentality as a squad was that it was all about the team and Gordon Strachan really helped develop that. I have to give credit to my teammates because I couldn't have scored that many goals without them, in particular my strike partner Brett Ormerod because he was a great foil for me.

During that season the goals bred confidence, which meant the lads were then looking to me even more to get the goals, that added a little bit more pressure but I used to love that."

## WORKING WITH STRACHAN

"It was brilliant working with Gordon Strachan, I still speak to him now and he is a top Manager that has shaped my career and even my thoughts now as a coach. I'm very lucky to have him as a sounding board.

In training there was always lots of fitness work especially in pre-season, but there was also a lot of technical work too. He knew the ability of the players he had and he knew how to manage them to get the best out of them.

He worked out the best way for us to get the results that we got and that put us on a real upward curve."

### FA CUP FINAL 2002 - 2003
"As a player you're always going to be disappointed if you don't win. I really enjoyed the build up, but the result of the game kind of diminished all that enjoyment.

The two week buildup to the final was brilliant, we got to do some amazing things which really brought the city together. It was great for the fans, but also for my family and my friends that came on the journey with us.

The Semi-Final was great at Villa Park, the fans were incredible, then when we got to Cardiff it was another level. I remember that sea of yellow and blue that was there, even though we lost and even after all the Arsenal fans had gone home, it was incredible.

From a personal perspective to have my dad there to see it after all he did for me and to have a lot of the family there was special, but ultimately I wanted to win. So the experience of the journey was amazing but the game and the result wasn't the best."

### SCORING v PORTSMOUTH
"It probably wasn't my best goal, but I think it's the goal that meant the most to the fans. It made sure we got one over on Portsmouth and it's always nice to score in a local derby. I don't think the Pompey fans will ever forget it either."

### BEATTIE'S BEST GOALS
"I think the free kick against Chelsea is one of my best and also the other one I scored after 14 seconds against them too. I got the ball, slipped in and I put the ball over Carlo

Cudicini. The half volley against West Bromwich Albion always sticks with me and the goal against Sunderland was also pretty special."

### BEATTIE MAKES HIS ENGLAND DEBUT v AUSTRALIA 12 FEBRUARY 2003

"I didn't really expect to get that far as a player, but looking back it was a great achievement and I am so glad that my dad saw me play for England.

The squad got announced and we had a training camp ahead of the games at Arsenal's training ground. We were training in the lead up to the game v Australia and Sven-Göran Eriksson just came up to me and said **'You're playing.'** It was a real honour to make my debut, we played at the Boleyn Ground and I made my debut in the same game as Wayne Rooney."

### MISSING OUT ON EURO 2004

"They were doing a documentary in the build up to Euro 2004 and it was around the time when there was some talk going about the players striking. England were filming at that time for a documentary about the build up to the Euros, I was involved along with Ashley Cole and Frank Lampard. I did some filming in my room telling them what was going on and after that I never played for England again. Emile Heskey got picked to go to the Euros ahead of me, but there's no doubt in my mind that I should have gone, but what can you do about it now."

### ON THE MOVE TO EVERTON

"I didn't really want to make the move, but Harry Redknapp came in and said **'You're my only saleable asset and I need to bring three or four more players'** and that was it. I was then free to go and speak to other clubs. I went and met David O'Leary who was at Aston Villa and David Moyes at Everton. Out of the two clubs I picked Everton and made the move in the January."

### CONNECTION WITH THE FANS

"I've always had a good relationship with the fans. I think primarily because they always saw that I put effort into the badge. I think that's the first thing fans want to see and then as a striker the goals are always going to help create that relationship too.

Since I left, I have always spoken well of the club, I see it as my home. I met my wife down there and the kids go to school in Southampton. Even when I was at my other clubs, I always had a good affinity with the city as I have a lot of friends and family down here.

I obviously always keep a close eye on how the clubs is doing. I was upset to see them slide down the leagues but then to come back the way they did was great. I'm sure it was a great journey for the fans, but also for the club to come through to the other side going in the right direction with the help of Markus Liebherr.

I enjoy going to St Mary's when I can, Southampton will always hold a dear place in my heart."

# DENNIS ROFE

1982 - 1984
**POSITION** : Defender
**APPS** : 25

**DEBUT:** 28/08/1982 v Coventry City

**SAINTS HONOURS:** 1983 - 1984 First Division Runner Up
**COACHING TEAM:** 1984 - 1991 / 1998 - 2005
**SAINTS COACHING HONOURS:** 2003 FA Cup Runner Up

A former Captain of Chelsea, Dennis Rofe joined Southampton in 1982 with Lawrie McMenemy signing him on a free transfer. Dennis made twenty appearances over a two year playing career before joining the coaching team in 1984. Starting off as reserve team coach, it wasn't long until he stepped up to the first team working alongside Chris Nicholl.

After brief spells at Bristol Rovers, Stoke and Fulham, Dennis returned to the Saints in 1998 as an academy coach before returning to the first team in 2001, this time working with Stuart Gray. Rofe would remain as Assistant Manager under Gordon Strachan and helped take Southampton to the 2003 FA Cup Final.

### ROFE BEGINS HIS SOUTHAMPTON CAREER
"I had been at Leicester and moved to Chelsea where I had spent two years. I picked up an injury near the end of my second season and the Manager assured me that I would get another contract. When the time came he said **'I'm not going to give you new contract, I'm going to let you go on a free transfer'**. At the time I was 32 and a neighbour who I lived next to up in Ash Vale, who was a Chelsea supporter, said **'Why don't you give Lawrie McMenemy a call'**. So I thought **'Why not I'll give him a ring.'** I rang the club's number and I got through to a lady and I asked if Lawrie McMenemy was available. To my

surprise she put me straight through, which I thought was a bit quick.

'Hello Denis' he said. I replied 'Hello Lawrie', to which he then asked 'Who's this?' I said 'Denis Rofe'. 'Oh they told me it was Denis Roach'. Denis Roach was a football agent and I half expected Lawrie to hang up, but luckily we carried on the conversation.

I explained what had happened and I was looking for a new club and wondering if there was an opportunity to join Southampton. He said **'Give me a little while to think about it.'** We spoke again a few weeks later and he said **'I tell you what I'll do, I'll give you three months...show me what you can do'**. Well that three months eventually turned into somewhere in the region of eighteen years.

I didn't play regularly but I would say Lawrie looked after me. We were in Europe at the time, he took me on all the trips and had treated me with utmost respect.

As a player I was privileged to be around when the three Wallace brothers played together. I remember the match when they all played together which for their family must have been phenomenal to see, three of their sons in the same team and they were really good guys too.

I was also lucky to be in the side that finished second in the first division in 1983 - 1984. There was lots of excitement because of what we had done, but I would say there was also a little bit of nerves thinking **'What have we now got to do next season?'** Around that time we had some really good European nights and it was a great time to be a Southampton player."

## FIRST STEPS INTO COACHING

"We were playing Everton at Arsenal in the Semi-Final of the FA Cup. I had been away with the reserves on the Wednesday at Millwall and Lawrie then said to myself and a couple of other players to get across to London and come to the team hotel for the Arsenal game on Saturday.

On the Friday he asked me if I could take the warm up and that was first time I had a clue that he was considering me for a coaching role. He told me to make it light hearted and take the pressure off the boys which I did. Unfortunately, we lost that game 2-1 but that was when I first had an inkling that it would be an open door for me if I wanted it.

I was approaching 34 and I had a knee injury which resulted in the loss of feeling in my left foot. Some said I lost it when I first started playing but that's another story. I had an operation to free the nerve and the doctor told me that feeling will come back, but it might take six months. So I thought '**I'm 34 I might as well retire**', and I did.

Frank Burrows was the reserve coach and when he left the club I was a bit part player, so I asked Lawrie if he would consider me for the reserves. Once again he said '**Just give me a little time to think about it**' and the answer was yes.

The transition into coaching was a gradual process in changing the relationships with players from teammate to coach. You certainly didn't want to go round stamping your feet saying '**Here I am listen to me!**' I found it a great learning curve and I always found that if you were honest with players and you treated them with respect, whether it was the top player or the youngest professional, and you understood their needs, then that was the key. I obviously made some mistakes, but I think the fact that I'd been there and done it as a player helped me a little bit."

## THE FIRST TEAM 1984 - 1991

"When Lawrie left, Chris Nicholl asked me if I would step up with him and Tony Barton at the first team, not long after that Tony left the club, so I was then number two with Chris. We had some marvellous cup runs, particularly in the League Cup where we thought we had a good chance but it didn't mature.

They were exciting days and it was the start of the Matt Le Tissier era. The Wallaces and Alan Shearer were coming along nicely and I can remember Alan Shearer's first game very clearly when he scored a hat-trick against Arsenal. It was a very special time."

## 1998 THE RETURN OF ROFE

"In my spell away I moved to Bristol Rovers as a coach initially, before having a spell as Manager. I really enjoyed doing that and at that time I also applied for a couple of other positions for Managerial jobs. But then when there was a chance to come back to Southampton I couldn't say no.

Initially I was in charge of a really good under eighteen's team, we had one or two players who I thought might go on and do a little bit better, but we had people like Chris Baird and Matthew Oakley coming through and they all became very good players.

It was a good time because in those days the Managers took an active part in watching the under 18's. Managers like Dave Jones and then later on Gordon Strachan would come out to Staplewood to watch the under 18's playing on Saturday morning before a first team game, which is something I wouldn't think happens too much these days. I really enjoyed my time with the youth team before I moved back to the first team."

## MOVING TO ST MARY'S

"When I first saw the site at St Mary's I thought **'How are they going to set a stadium on there?'** but they did. I think you worried that when you came from a small enclosed ball of fire that was The Dell, to a new big open stadium, teams would come for their revenge. Teams didn't like coming to The Dell, like Manchester United we had a few great results against them. But it all went very well to be honest, it was a great move for the club as things were moving forward. We had a new stadium, the training ground was expanding at Staplewood and the club was making progress which was really good."

## ROFE v GRAEME SOUNESS - 25th OCTOBER 2003

"Well I put it down to the fact I wanted to win and he wanted to win. To be honest he misheard me, because he thought I was trying to get Andy Cole sent off and I wasn't trying to do that at all. I remember correctly my words were **'If the referee has seen that, they will send him off'** but Graeme reacted as he did and that's what happens in football. I mean Graeme was lucky that there were seven stewards holding me back. But in all seriousness, those things happen in football. I certainly have absolutely no problem if I met Graeme again and I'm sure he'd be the same."

# THE FA CUP - 2003

"As you progress in the competition you begin to dream big. I always remember we were at the training ground listening to the Semi-Final draw and it came out that Arsenal had drawn Sheffield United. All the players roared because we had avoided Arsenal and drawn Watford and that's not being disrespectful to Watford in anyway, but Gordon leapt up and shouted '**You sit down and shut up...Don't you go thinking you are at Cardiff already!**' He was just very anxious to keep the place calm and focussed.

It was a wonderful feeling that Semi-Final, it was at Villa Park and when the coach pulled in towards the stadium all I could see was yellow shirts and I thought '**We haven't got any supporters, where are they?**' And then as we turned the corner all you could see was red and white and it was the most magnificent sight. That feeling was only beaten by when we got the result and the referee blew the final whistle. It was a magnificent feeling us all knowing that we were going to the FA Cup Final.

We went up to Cardiff on the Thursday and we trained on the Friday morning. I can't remember too much about the training session, but people were naturally excited and we had to calm the emotions a little bit. During that week we tried to make it as normal as possible so that the players were comfortable. You obviously spent a bit of time sorting things out like tickets for the family and a few other bits, but the most important thing was the game and I don't think we could've prepared any better. If my memory serves me correctly we had a full complement of players. There wasn't anybody that was missing and for people like Chris Marsden and James Beattie it was their first Cup final, as it was for most of us, but it was such was an exciting time.

In the FA Cup Final itself, I felt we played reasonably well but not as well as I thought we could have done. We had a chance to score before they did and we didn't and we ended up losing 1-0 and everybody was really disappointed. We felt we were at full tilt holding Arsenal but that didn't really give us a chance to express what we could do.

At full time so often the fans of the losing teams get out as quickly as they can, but not the Southampton fans. I remember it was the Arsenal fans that were leaving. When we did our lap of honour at the end to see all of the Saints fans still in their seats applauding us was a really moving few moments. Who knows what they would had done if we had won. I think the fans would have still been there now!

Every time I come off the M4 for Newbury as you come down the slip road I always remember that journey back on the Sunday. I still get the feeling I'm still sitting in front of that coach whenever I drive down it in my car. The reason it was so significant is because at that point we were on the home straight back to St Mary's and when we got there, the amount of people that were waiting for us and welcomed us back was really incredible. The support was amazing and the fans were a credit to the club."

## EUROPEAN ADVENTURE 2003 -2004
"We felt that we let ourselves down a little bit in Europe. We drew the Romanian side Steaua Bucharest and drew 1-1 at home. We lost away and we were a bit disappointed with that, we felt we let ourselves down."

## WORKING WITH THE RISING STARS - LE TISSIER AND SHEARER
"The big two names I remember would be Alan Shearer and Matt Le Tissier. I remember going to Guernsey to look at Matt and when he came over we played at Eastleigh. Matt was fifteen or sixteen at the time and he was running rings around everyone. In fact, he came from a very good footballing family as well because his brothers were pretty decent players too. Matt could do things that other people just couldn't do. He was never a fitness fanatic, in fact he came to me once when we started doing some organised warm ups and said '**Coach can I have word? I don't like these organised warm ups.**' To which I replied '**As long as you keep scoring goals Matt you can do whatever you want**'.

A lot of things that people take for granted are things like the penalties and the free kicks he used to work on day after day. So much so that we had a goalkeeper called Tim Flowers and Matt would take penalties against him and say '**Tim I'm going to put this one low to your right**' and sure enough bang. Tim Flowers never got anywhere near it and in the end Tim said '**No I'm not doing anymore of this, you get a reserve goalkeeper in**'.

Alan Shearer, right from day one, wanted to be the best player he could be, he had a real determination and he was not afraid to berate someone. If they got down the line and didn't cross the ball, as young as he was at seventeen, he would give them what for.

Dave Merrington had Matt and Alan in the youth team to start with. He used to come back and I would ask how they got on and Dave would say **'Won 9-0, Shearer scored 4, Le Tissier got the other 5'**. Shearer would stay out for hours practicing his finishing and Matt would practice free kicks for as long as he could, they were a joy to work with really.

There were so many terrific players though that I got to work with: Wayne Bridge and Francis Benali at left back and Jason Dodd at right back. Chris Marsden was a very good player for the team and a good player for the club. If something wasn't right before the Manager and myself could get dressing room, you would hear Chris going **'Oi you, come on you're better than that. Get going'**. James Beattie up front scored some great goals with sheer effort and determination. He would just get on the end of things in the box.

When I first started we had a centre back called Russell Osman and after training Russell would stay out with whoever wanted to stay out playing both with his right and left foot. In the end I would have to call him in everyday and that's what all those players were like. It was a joy to work with them."

## THE MANAGERS

"Let's start with Lawrie McMenemy. Lawrie was the Manager of the club. Managers today look after the first team but Lawrie looked after the club and nobody came to work at Southampton unless Lawrie said so. Those days have gone but he was very good at what he did. He was excellent in the transfer market at persuading players to join and getting another mile out of them.

Chris Nicholl was decent. Southampton was his first managerial job and he achieved quite a bit of success and he was great to work with.

Gordon Strachan, I loved working with Gordon. He wanted and demanded the best out of every player and didn't suffer fools gladly. He had a fiery temperament just like he had when he played. He went on to manage Scotland and I really enjoyed the time with him and Garry Pendrey, that was a real icing on the cake for me to work with them both."

## REMEMBERING GEORGE HORSFALL

"When I first started there was a guy at the club, who is no longer with us, George Horsfall. When we were doing the reserves we didn't have a kit man and we used to have to pack the kit and the boots and George used to say '**You go home, I will pack your skip don't worry it will all be right.**' George used to always give you wise words and I learnt a lot from him. He was a tremendous man and he was dedicated to Southampton and people like him are sorely missed in the game."

## THE DELL

"I loved the Dell. It was always absolutely buzzing, it was crammed, people singing loudly and I remember children being passed down the front and put over the wall to watch the game. The atmosphere when you came out the tunnel and walked to the dugouts was electric. The Dell was feared by the majority of clubs and because of that intimate close feeling and I loved it."

## WRITTEN IN THE STARS - LE TISSIER'S FINAL GOAL AT THE DELL

"I remember that game and when we put Matt on Stuart Gray said '**You know he will score the last goal here**' and sure enough he did."

## ROFE ON SOUTHAMPTON

"Southampton has always been a club that gave me a chance when I needed it and I think I'm the only person that has been back three times in some guise, so I must have been doing something right, not too sure what it was though! I enjoyed my time at the club and Southampton is still my home. I get to games whenever I can and my son is still a season ticket holder.

Since I've left, there has been a bit of up and down, but the tide has turned and let's hope there's bigger and better things on the horizon."

# DAVID PUCKETT

1977 - 1986
POSITION : Forward
APPS : 59
GOALS: 16

DEBUT: 17/03/1981 v Everton

SAINTS HONOURS: 1983 - 1984 First Division Runner Up
SOUTHAMPTON ACADEMY: 1997 - 2010

Born and raised in Southampton, David Puckett joined the Saints in 1977 having played schoolboy football throughout his junior footballing years. David would go on to make 94 appearances for the club, but was a regular name on the team sheet appearing as a substitute over one hundred times. Puckett was also part of the 1983 - 1984 squad that finished second in the league and reached the Semi-Final of the FA Cup. After his playing career, David returned to Southampton and took on a role with the Academy coaching some of the greatest names to come through the club in recent times from Theo Walcott to Gareth Bale.

## PUCKETT BECOMES A SAINT

"Officially I became a Saint when I left school and signed as an apprentice, but I like to think that really it started a long time before that being a Southampton boy born and bred.

I remember growing up and my mum and dad encouraging me and my brothers Julian and Graeme to just play sport. We would be out for hours in Edwina Close playing heads and volleys against the wall. I can remember from a young age always doing lots of keep-ups and could do hundreds and to this very day I still do a hundred a day.

In all the teams I grew up playing for I was always the top scorer and at three of them I remember we won the treble. During that period, I was also picked for Southampton schoolboys to play for the under eleven's, so I was wearing the Southampton stripes even as a ten year old.

I went on to represent the Saints at every age group growing up and once you were in those sides, scouts from the club would come and watch you. So if you were good enough there was a real chance that they would be interested in signing you.

Tom Parker who played for Arsenal and England was one of the scouts. My dad was an Arsenal fan and knew who he was so it was nice when he approach my mum and dad to say that the club were very interested in me, and that when I was fourteen they would be most probably looking to sign me. When I got to fourteen it was Bill Ellerington who came to my house to get me to sign the forms. As soon as I was old enough the forms were signed and that meant I could go and have a weekly training session at The Dell. We would train in the gymnasium which was under the old west stand and I got to play with the current apprentices and other potential players like myself.

At sixteen I was offered the chance to sign apprentice professional forms for the club. It didn't take me a split second to say yes. My parents had said to me before that though, that I had to get as many O-Levels as I could and if I did they would agree to me signing. I think we were always going to sign, but it was good way of making sure I stayed focused at school.

Myself and Mark Whitlock signed our forms on the same day and we ended up playing together from the age of 14 right up until we were thirty. We both then left in the same week and both went to Bournemouth. We both left there at the same time too and played together at Aldershot. We ended up playing in veterans football together too, so mine and Mark's career mirrored each other quite well."

### BREAKING INTO THE FIRST TEAM
"The way it was done in my time was that when you were a youth team player you got ready on a daily basis in the reserve team dressing room. The first team squad of players

all got changed in the home dressing room and then we would all go and train together.

As an apprentice you had to go into the home team dressing room to give out the kit and the boots because you had players to look after. I was assigned Phil Boyer, Nick Holmes and David Peach initially and of course I had to clean my own boots as well. Your job was to make sure they had all their kit on time and exactly how they wanted it. Then after the session you would have to go in and pick up the dirty kit and clean those boots again. You had to be respectful of the players in the first team dressing room but also that was the dressing room I wanted to get into. You couldn't be shy, you had to go in there full of confidence because with all the senior players that were there at the time, if they saw you were shy they would test you out a little bit, so you had to be strong character.

I first got picked for the reserves to be a sub but about an hour before the kick off Oshor Williams had failed a fitness test. I remember him coming over to me and telling that I was now going to be playing and a young lad was going to come over to take my place on the bench.

He handed me the number seven shirt and said '**You're playing now so whatever I do, don't do and whatever I don't do, do and you will be alright.**'

We won 2-1 and I scored both goals and scoring on my reserve debut with such short notice was pretty special and few years later I did exactly the same and scored two on my first team debut.

With the first team, I had travelled on a number of pre-season tours around that time. I used to get a few minutes here and there, which was nice to help me get used to travelling with the team and being around the set up.

I used to be sub in the days when it was only one substitute and in-fact over my career I was picked as a Saints first team sub over one hundred times, which I think was a record. I also got on in fifty two of those games which was another record for the times of just one substitute. It was great to be part of it but of course you wished you could have been starting, but I think myself incredibly lucky to have been picked to be on the bench for my boyhood club, so you have to look at it both ways."

## FULL DEBUT HOME v ARSENAL

"My first team full debut came when I was picked to play away from home against West Ham and my full home debut was against Arsenal which is a memorable game for me as I scored two. At the game v Arsenal I got called up in a very similar way to how it happened for the reserves.

I knew I was in the squad and was expecting to be on the bench but in the week leading up to the game we knew Steve Moran had been carrying an injury and was almost certain not to feature, but we didn't know who would step in. An hour before the game Lawrie McMenemy threw me the number nine shirt and said **'You're playing'**.

There was no real instruction or tactics or anything. I think one of the Manager's strengths in terms of man management was that he put a side together that was full of quality, experienced professionals like Mick Mills, Dave Watson, Alan Ball, Nick Holmes, Mick Channon and Kevin Keegan, and then he would work the younger players around them. They would look out for you and make sure you were ok. So it was never a real risk putting one of the younger players in. We trained the first team so I knew the lads and Lawrie obviously felt I was ready and good enough to step up.

I got myself ready for the game and was in the centre circle ready for kick off stood next to Kevin Keegan. Just as the referee was about to blow his whistle Keegan turned to me and said **'An hour ago he said the Manager asked me who I wanted to play up front with today, you or George Lawrence ... I said YOU, don't let me down!'**

So five seconds into my debut I was processing what Kevin had just said thinking **'Blimey it was Kevin Keegan who said he wanted me to play with him, I better not let him down'**.

We won the game 3-1. I set up the first goal for David Armstrong and scored the other two, so I think it's fair to say I don't think I let him down. I remember the Milton Road end that day which is where I stood as a kid. When I scored the two goals I just remember hearing the roar from the crowd and realising that was for me and the team. It was an incredible sight and I can still picture it now.

In the game I got injured and damaged my ankle ligaments so ended up being out for a while after. The adrenalin of the game and keeping it moving got me through the ninety minutes, but I left the ground after my home debut on crutches."

## 1983- 1984 RUNNERS UP IN THE LEAGUE

"To be in the side for the 83-84 season was incredible and I got a run in the side towards the end. Being part of those final games where we needed to get those extra wins and to be in the side when we finished second was very special.

I remember the final game against Notts County, it was away and it was a game we knew we had to win to secure second place. Back in those days there was only two sets of each kit, one long sleeved and one short sleeved and that was it for the season. So whoever was in that number for that particular game had that shirt, you didn't have your own kit like today. On the last day of the season you normally got to keep the shirt as you would be getting a new set next season.

On that final game I knew I was playing and I knew that I was number nine. So I was thinking **'This is fantastic, we're going to be runners up, I'm playing for my hometown team and I'm going to get the shirt at the end of the game'**.

Then at full time Lawrie McMenemy said **'You see all those travelling fans, go and throw your shirts into the crowd. They have supported you all season'**. My heart sank, I obviously realised what he was saying and as a fan I would have wanted the players to throw their shirts into the crowd… but as a player I didn't want to say goodbye to my shirt. I reluctantly took it off and threw it into the crowd.

Fast forward twenty years to when I was at the academy and in my office I got a note on the desk saying **'Please call this number. I've got something of yours'**.

I called the number and the lady said she had something of mine, could I go and meet her. It turned out she was in the crowd at Notts County and caught my shirt and she said **'I think it's about time you had it back if you would like it?'** So I got her a signed shirt from the Saints team at the time and a huge bunch of flowers and swapped shirts. I had got my number nine shirt back, which is a very special memento for me of that very special season."

## ALAN BALL'S BLAZER

'We were on a pre-season tour and I was one of the many young lads who was on this particular trip. We were heading to Ireland to play Limerick and when we were at the airport Alan Ball was there with a few of the senior players. He came over to us young players to have a chat.

During the conversation he said '**I have had this jacket a long time now, whoever it fits can have it.**' Rueben Agboola tried it on, Mark Whitlock and a few more lads who were too tall and a few who were carrying a few extra pounds and it didn't fit them. So it got to me, I tried it on and it fitted perfectly. So Alan said '**Right, it's yours**'. I didn't really think any more of it, he put the jacket back on and carried on wearing it on the trip. At the start of the season we were away at Coventry and we had travelled up on the Friday night and I was roomed with Alan Ball.

Rooming with Alan Ball on its' own was pretty special for me as a young lad, one of the experienced pros and a World Cup winner. I was thinking about all the questions I could ask him when we were in the room. In the room, he had two suit bags and I thought it was just the suit for the game. He passed one to me and said '**I have had this dry cleaned for you**'. It was the jacket and it was now mine.

I used to wear it a lot and always kept it. A couple of years back there was a memorial dinner at St Mary's to mark ten years since he sadly passed away and I wore the jacket. I told this story for the first time and you could hear a pin drop in the room. His two daughters were there and they didn't have a clue and when they heard the story they came over and we had a big hug. It was a very special moment, it felt like a piece of Alan was in the room and they got to hug their dad's jacket. I'm so glad I still have it, Alan was a very special person."

## IVAN GOLAC

"One player that I did get on very well with in the first team and someone I loved as a person and a player was Ivan Golac. He was one of the best players I ever played with.

Those that trained with him will know what I'm talking about, in terms of his one touch play he was quite exceptional. I used to love training in The Dell gym with him and the first team. On a Friday before a game the training session would be a five-a-side. It would be the ten outfield players who were going to be playing the following day, and there was always someone nursing a knock that would rest instead of joining the session, so as sub I got to play most of the time.

I remember Ivan was the best player in the gym along with Alan Ball every single week. The way that he played rubbed off big time on me and it was a pleasure to be in his company."

### FAN MAIL FOR KEEGAN

"We had some big names in the side at the time and one of them was obviously Kevin Keegan. If we had training at ten he would get in at nine, as it would take him an hour to get in the car park because there would be so many fans waiting for autographs. He was great with the fans and would never turn anyone away.

It was a great example to us younger players to never turn down a request to sign anything, but it did mean we didn't get to spend much time with him socially as he would be in and out of the dressing room to get on the training pitch on time.

The likes of Mark Whitlock, Rueben Agboola, Steve Baker and myself who were apprentices, would get what we thought was fan mail for us. At the time, Keegan would get sacks full of letters and we were over the moon with our handful. Once we opened ours though we realised they weren't really for us as they would all say '**Can you get Kevin Keegan to sign this for me?**'"

### FAVOURITE GOALS

"The record books say that I scored sixteen goals for the Saints but I scored about twenty in friendlies and over eighty for the reserves as well, so I see myself having scored more than just the sixteen for Saints. All my goals were very special to me and to score winning goals against Arsenal at home twice and then Tottenham at home twice will always stick with me. One of the games v Spurs was a 1-0 win and I scored a header in the top corner which was a pretty good finish.

I have got videos of all my goals for Southampton. At the time when I played, the club did VHS video recordings of the games and they would have someone sat up in the gantry at The Dell with a camera. They were done more for records for the club or if the Manager wanted to use them for coaching points. Often I would ask to borrow it the week after if I had scored and I would make out I wanted to watch it for tactics but I was getting it so I could take copies of my goals and make my own tape."

## MOVING ON AFTER NINE YEARS
"Being in the squad every year in my time at the club was very special but I never really established myself in the starting lineup and I wasn't playing in as many games as I wanted to be. Looking back on my career I now realise I was a young lad with world class players. I had the opportunity to train and play with them week in week out and in hindsight I was very privileged to play with such great players and be part of those teams.

There was always quality coming into the club and being a forward player I was so lucky to be playing games with players like Joe Jordan, Frank Worthington, Charlie George and Alan Curtis.

When it got to 1986 I realised that it was time for me to make a move and get regular first team football. I had been offered a new improved two year contract, but I turned it down. I really didn't want to leave Saints but I knew I had to, I had given it nine seasons to try and become a regular in the side but the time had come for a new challenge."

## COACHING THE FUTURE SOUTHAMPTON STARS: PUCKETT JOINS THE ACADEMY
"I returned to Southampton in 2003 to work with the Academy, it was a tremendous second career for me and I thoroughly enjoyed it. I worked every age group in my time working at the club and went from working in the development centre to being youth team coach.

All the players that I coached that made it into the first team were good enough to get into the first team not because of me, but because of their ability. I was very lucky to have worked with some fantastic players including Gareth Bale, Theo Walcott, Adam Lallana, Tyrone Mings, James Ward-Prowse, Luke Shaw, Alex Oxlade-Chamberlain and Calum Chambers, and I even tried to sign Mason Mount before he went to Chelsea.

I knew them all from when they were very young and I knew all of their families too. One thing they all had in common was the hunger and their desire to make it, which was just like I was at their age. I feel very privileged to have worked with them and help them in a very small way in their journey. I find myself now at weekends not only looking for the Saints results but also the scores of the games featuring the hundreds of players I have worked with. Looking out to see how they are getting on at clubs from Wycombe Wanderers to Real Madrid."

## PLAYING FOR MY HOME TOWN

"I have got a picture of when I was eight years old getting my first medal when I was playing for my Cub side and I was wearing the red and white stripes. To then grow up wearing the red and white every year in a representative side unit I made the first team was incredibly special. I know that I have worn the number eleven shirt in every age group from under ten to the first team for Southampton, it was always the club I wanted to play for and I didn't want to be travelling anywhere else to play. I knew I was good enough and I had this belief that I could do it.

The thing that you don't know growing up, was what it would be like stepping into that first team and what it would be like playing at The Dell in front of 30,000 people. Could you do it when it came to the big stage and not let the pressure get to you? For me it was something I couldn't wait to find out and when I did it I loved every second."

# LIFE OF A SAINT

# GLENN COCKERILL

**1985 - 1994**
**POSITION** : Midfield
**APPS** : 340
**GOALS:** 39

**DEBUT:** 19/10/1985 v Luton Town

**SAINTS HONOURS** : 86-87 Player of the Season, 1992 Zenith Data Cup Runner Up

Joining Southampton in the October of 1985, Glenn Cockerill was one of Chris Nicholl's first signings having taken over the reins from Lawrie McMenemy. Glenn signed from Sheffield United where he had scored ten goals in sixty two games.

A skillful midfielder, he cemented his place as the heart midfield for the Saints and made 358 performances in his nine years at the club. Captain Cockerill took over the armband from Jimmy Case and led out the Saints at the 1992 Zenith Date Cup Final. Southampton took on a Nottingham Forest side full of big names and came close to victory, but it wasn't to be and Glenn was denied the chance of being only the second Captain to lift silverware for the club at the old Wembley. Glenn stayed at the club until December 1993 when he moved to Leyton Orient.

### CHRIS NICHOLL'S FIRST SIGNING

"Someone said to me that Jon Gittens also signed on the same day, but I can't remember seeing him when I signed. I do remember the day very well though, I was playing for Sheffield United and Luton had been chasing me for so long. I had been chatting to David Pleat nearly every Sunday for six months and he was desperate to sign me. So it was ironic that my debut for Southampton would come against Luton.

I spoke to a few people like Graham Taylor, he was my first ever Manager in the league when he signed me for Lincoln from the Non-League in 1976. I had always been in contact with him as he tried to sign me a few times. First for Watford when I was still at Lincoln and later on when I was at Southampton for Aston Villa. He was the one who said I should go to Southampton, I remember him saying **'You don't really play on that plastic pitch at Luton'**. A few of the older professionals I knew also said Southampton was the club to go to and I didn't look back."

### THE DEBUT v LUTON
"As I said, it was ironic that Luton was my first game. I remember we got hammered 7-0 and before the end of the game I was thinking **'What have I done here?'**

I signed on the Wednesday and in those days the FA would let you train on the plastic pitch, we did that on the Thursday and that was my first session with the team.

I played upfront with Steve Moran that day, I had played upfront before so didn't feel out of my depth, but Luton were just so good that day and we were very poor. From that day forward though things just turned around and we went on a really good run after that game. That year went on to get to the FA Cup Semi-Final and in those first four years we really should have won something. We were a really good team, we had a lot of lads like Jimmy Case, David Armstrong and Danny Wallace. Plus we also had Matt Le Tissier and Francis Benali that were coming through."

### CASE AND COCKERILL: THE ROCKS IN THE MIDDLE OF THE PARK
"I remember when I signed Chris Nicholl said to me **'I'm bringing you in to replace Jimmy Case'**. So it's ironic that me and Jimmy ended up together for six years and we did so well together creating a real bond. Jimmy was a few years older than me but it just seemed to work. I think what hit it all off was the meeting the next day after the Luton game.

Chris Nicholl pulled us all in on the Sunday morning, we had a really long meeting and he had a go at a few of the older players and proper laid down the law. I got away with it a bit as I had just signed, but he certainly told a few of the senior players they weren't doing enough. It was a bit of an eye opener for me having just met all the lads and joined the club. After the meeting everyone left and it was just me and Jimmy who remained. Jimmy looked up at me and said **'Has he finished?'** I replied **'Yes Jimmy'** and he said **'Good, what you doing, fancy a pint?'** and from that moment on we got on like a house on fire. I rented a flat on Dibden Bridge and within a month he moved in with myself and Gerry Forrest.

We got on really well on and off the pitch. On the pitch, not many players got the better of us and we complimented each other so well. I did the running and closing down and if I was struggling I could just give Jimmy the ball. He was great for me and taught me so much."

## 1986-1987 PLAYER OF THE SEASON

"I was runner up in the 1985 - 1986 season, Peter Shilton won it that year and I was lucky enough to win it the season after. When I played at Sheffield United I was starting to hit my peak and maybe that's what Chris Nicholl saw in me. When I arrived at Southampton at twenty six years old I was hitting my peak, I was fit and I didn't really have poor game. I might have had a poor game with the ball but I gave my all in every match. The team were playing well, me and Jimmy were playing well together and that season and I scored a few long range goals, so maybe all that added together helped clinch me the Player of the Year. I was so pleased though, my first full year in the top flight to win supporters Player of the Year, it meant a lot."

## CAPTAIN COCKERILL

"I loved captaining the Saints and I got given the armband when Jimmy Case left. There were probably three of us that could have been up for it. In my eyes it was between me, Neil Ruddock (who were experienced members of the team) or Alan Shearer who was up and coming but such a good leader. I knew I could do it, I felt like the lads looked up to me and respected me. So maybe that's what did it for the Manager. I learnt so much playing alongside Jimmy, he was a great Captain and that rubbed off on me.

I think I was the right choice, not because I was the best player but because of the respect that I had at the club. So when Ian Branfoot asked me to be the Captain I was delighted because it meant a lot to lead out the side."

## ZENITH DATA CUP FINAL - 29TH MARCH 1992

"We got close to getting to Wembley in my first season when we got to the Semi-Final of the FA Cup, but we finally got there in 1992 for the Zenith Date Cup Final. It was a great honour for me to captain the club and lead them out at Wembley and we couldn't have got any closer to lifting the trophy.

Nottingham Forest were a very good team with the likes of Stuart Pearce, Roy Keane, Teddy Sherringham, Scot Gemmill, Des Walker and of course the legend that was Brian Clough as their Manager.

We were a new team getting to know each other as Ian Branfoot was now the Manager, but you could go through our team and we still had great quality players like Tim Flowers, Neil Ruddock, Matt Le Tissier and Alan Shearer. So the names on that team sheet for that final for both sides was pretty incredible.

We were 2-0 down and had a really poor first half. In the second half though we made a real fight of it. Ian Branfoot didn't make any substitutes at half time which surprised me, but in the dressing room he fired us up **'Come on you lot, you know you're all better than that!'** So second half we dug in and we got back to 2-2. Matt Le Tissier and Kevin Moore scored. I remember we nearly won it in the last minute. Terry Hurlock had a brilliant shot saved. It was going top corner and I thought it was in. I almost turned to celebrate but somehow the keeper tipped it out. The game went to extra time and sadly Nottingham Forest found a winner.

It was obviously disappointing not to win, but it was a fantastic day and for me to lead the team out was very special moment in my career. The fans were brilliant that day too, they were unbelievable. The thing about Southampton fans is that they are a team in the stands and they become part of the team on the pitch. They had their ups and downs about the Manager at the time, but they always supported the side. In that final they proved that, they could see the effort that we were putting in and they were terrific all throughout the whole match.

When we went back to the hotel afterwards we were all gutted and disappointed for the fans who had turned out in their numbers. I'm on the Saints Archive and the fans still talk about that game and it's amazing. It feels like they talk about it in the same way they do about the 1976 final and that's really special for me."

## APPEARANCES

"I stayed at Matt Le Tissier's house a couple of years ago and he has a book with all the appearances and stats in it and he got it out and said **'Skip, have you seen your appearances for the first five years?'** And it was something like 50, 51, 52, 50, 51 games in each season.

I was very lucky with injuries which I didn't get, I had the odd suspension now and again but not that many. I was just one of those players that just wanted to play and I was never tired. I see players talking about being tired these days and I just don't get it. Around two hundred and fifty games in five years is frightening really, especially now some don't do one hundred and fifty in five years. I just wanted to play though and I kept that mentality up right until I retired at thirty nine."

## COCKERILL ON THE MOVE

"I didn't really want to leave Southampton. I had been offered another year contract for my testimonial year, but I was in and out of the team towards the end. The Premier League was getting a bit too quick for me and from the age of seventeen I had always been playing every Saturday. I didn't like the thought of not playing and I just wanted to keep going.

Leyton Orient came in for me along with Derby and I decided to go to Orient, but I had a great time at Southampton and I was gutted to leave."

## THE FANS

"The Saints fans are brilliant, and were amazing to me. Maybe because I got off to such a good start, I came in towards the start of the season and it was only October I think when I signed for the club, so I nearly had a full season. Take away the first game after that we did ok, I scored on my home debut at The Dell in the League. I remember we played QPR and I won 3-0 with Danny Wallace scoring the other two. From that point I was off and running.

I think the fans appreciated me not because I was the best player in the world but because of my commitment to the cause. I was so lucky to have played with some very good players when I was at the club and then the young kids coming through were exceptional.

I was very lucky to have played for Southampton when I did and I feel very lucky to still get a lovely reception even when I go back now."

# RUEBEN AGBOOLA

1980 - 1985
POSITION : Defender
APPS : 111

DEBUT: 29/11/1980 v Manchester United

SAINTS HONOURS : 1983 - 1984 First Division Runner Up

Rueben Agboola joined the Southampton Youth set up in 1978 before signing his professional contract and making his debut v Manchester United at Old Trafford in the same game as Danny Wallace. It was the 1982 season when he really established himself in the first team and went on to make ninety appearances for the Saints. 1983 saw Rueben cement his place in Lawrie McMenemy's squad as a sweeper and was a key part of the team that reached the FA Cup Semi Final and finished second in the First Division that season.

Rueben left Southampton in 1985 going on to play for Sunderland, Charlton, Port Vale, Swansea and Woking. He also played nine times for Nigeria including playing in the 1992 Africa Cup of Nations.

### LONDON BOY BECOMES A SAINT

"Growing up I always played up an age for my local team, so I was playing under twelves at the age of nine. I remember when I was thirteen I was sub for the mens first team and we played Dagenham in the cup, so from a young age I was always playing ahead of myself.

One of the coaches in the older youth teams had a connection with Southampton in London and he said **'I think you are ready to have a trial'**. So he arranged for me to go to their

London selection centre and I went along for two or three weeks. Prior to that, I had trials with West Ham, but nothing really came of that. I trained with Southampton for a few weeks and I was lucky enough to be taken on and that's how my journey with the club began.

In 1978 I signed as an apprentice when I left school and came straight down to Southampton. In the early days you were in the youth team and you had to work up to the reserves. You would play against mens teams like Portsmouth Royal Navy and other local teams like Netley, that was the first stepping stone before getting into the reserves.

As an apprentice you had to clean all the boots along with loads of other little tasks but the main thing was to train hard and do what you could to impress.

I had about six players to look after as an apprentice when it came to cleaning their boots and sorting their kit. One of the main players I had was Chris Nicholl and a big thing for us was Christmas bonus from the players, so you all wanted a player who paid well when they got allocated.

I remember in my first year I cleaned Chris's boots and it was getting close to the end of the day on the last training before Christmas. He still hadn't paid me and everyone was asking if he had. At this point I was thinking '**He's going to bump me and not give me a bonus**'. Then just as he was about to walk out of the changing room he tapped me on the shoulder and said '**I haven't paid you your Christmas bonus yet have I? What's the most someone has got so far?**'

I lied and told him it was £5.00 more than it actually was! He then put an extra £5.00 on top of that it, so I did quite well that year in the end.

When I did my second year as an apprentice we were put into pairs and Ian Juryeff was my partner. I was in charge of the apprentices and I used to hand out all the jobs. I used to take the easy ones or the jobs that had already been done. I would be sat there and Ian would be like '**What are you sat down with a cup of tea you haven't got time for that?**' To which I would reply that, my areas hadn't been used since Tuesday and it had been done already earlier in the week!"

## MANCHESTER UNITED AWAY: THE LONDON BOYS MAKE THIER DEBUT

"It was in the second year that me and Danny Wallace made our debuts. We had known each other for years having been in London together, but he was a few years younger than me. We found out in the dressing room that we were going to be playing about ten to two.

We got to the ground and normally we would be expected to put the kit out, they sent everyone out of the changing room and me and Danny sat there waiting to do our jobs and then Lawrie just said **'And you two, get out there, go and see what it's all about, you could be playing out there one day'**.

So we went out and had a little look around, came back in and Lawrie started his team talk. I was sat next to Danny and I heard my name mentioned, we both looked at each other and thought **'He's got that wrong'**. Then we heard Danny's name mentioned and again we both looked at each other and McMenemy said **'Yes you're both playing!'**

He continued his talk and gospel truth he said to the team **'Go out there and treat it like a practice match. Doesn't matter if you win, lose or draw. If we lose I will just blame these two kids.'** We couldn't believe it and we didn't really have time to think about it, we weren't even used to playing with the first team in training so we were right in at the deep end. It was very special to make my debut with Danny. With us both being black, both from London and both pretty new to it all. Normally your debut is something you do on your own, so to share that experience with someone else is pretty rare.

Nobody knew anything about us, even our own fans. My mate was in the stand and he couldn't believe it as I had seen him a few days before and obviously not said anything because I didn't know.

I thought I did ok in the game, I remember tackling Garry Birtles and he was known for being a very hard player. So I put a strong tackle in and he stayed down. I was thinking **'I hardly touched him'**. He got back up and I tackled him again and that time he went off. I remember thinking that I thought that that level was going to be much harder than it was. Having played just a few reserve games, I thought these guys were invincible, but obviously not.

The noise inside Old Trafford was incredible, I had never heard noise like it. My ears were still ringing after the game. You couldn't even talk to someone five yards away from you on the pitch it was that loud. The game felt like it was all in slow motion and then all of a sudden it was over, but it's certainly a day I will never forget."

## THREE AT THE BACK WITH AGBOOLA IN THE MIDDLE

"When I initially got into the team I fitted in at the back in a kind of three. When we played away I used to sit behind covering Chris Nicholl and Dave Watson with anything over the top and then at home I would be just in-front doing all the running for Alan Ball. I wasn't playing too frequently initially and I wasn't really playing sweeper at that point. I was more of a midfielder. I remember I could just kick a ball out of defence without looking because I knew where Danny Wallace would be. We had a great understanding. If I needed a get out ball that was the pass, I could knock it long and he would be there.

After a couple of years we got the nucleus right with Mark Wright and Nick Holmes in the middle with me, Mark Dennis on the left and Mick Mills on the right and then in front of us there was always quality with players."

## 1983 - 1984

"We had the cup run that year along with our performance in the league. I think initially we kind of fell into being contenders for the title and we didn't really expect it. We kept chipping away at each match and as we got to Christmas we were still up there.

All of a sudden teams started to play differently against us, you knew they were changing their pattern of play because they were scared that we were pretty much invincible at that stage. We were winning away and at home we hardly lost. We always felt we could win; we could be 3-0 down and we just knew that we could create chances and get back into a game. If a goal went in against us it didn't matter because we knew we could go down the other end and score.

We found that we didn't concede goals late on either because we were such a fit young team. So we didn't have to worry too much about our legs going towards the end of games.

I always thought we were a confident side. Without being cocky, we hadn't won any trophies but when you're winning match after match you do feel invincible.

The Semi-Final defeat was a real low in such a great season for me. We should have gone all the way and you know we could have won the league too and done the double that season quite easily, but it's easy to say that when you look back. Regardless of that, what a season it was."

### GLENN HODDLE CHALLENGE

"We were playing at White Hart Lane and my instruction that game was to mark Glenn Hoddle man to man. I was playing in midfield and I had a couple of little bites at him early in the game. The next time the ball came to him I was a bit slow off the mark. He got to the ball and expected me to be there, he flicked the ball on and I came in slightly late but didn't really make contact.

He just landed on me really but he had twisted his knee and was stretchered off after four minutes having torn his knee ligaments. In his book, apparently the worst tackle of his career was by me, but like I said I didn't really even touch him and I didn't even get booked. I remember the next eighty six minutes were quite interesting as everyone wanted a bit of me. I went to left back and at one stage Steve Perryman split my shin pad.

That night I had loads of family in the stands and my old school headteacher. It was the first time for most of them to see me play and they couldn't work out why everyone was booing me every time I got the ball. Obviously the injury to Hoddle wound up the Spurs fans up that night."

### PLAYING WITH THE BEST

"We had such a great wealth of experience and you can't take away from Lawrie how good he was at bringing those players to the club. There is that famous quiz question about the former England Captains, **'Which side had 6 in one team'**, that was us. Mick Channon, Dave Watson, Peter Shilton, Kevin Keegan, Mick Mills and Alan Ball all in our team, you certainly won't ever have that again and having those players in the side was invaluable.

I remember Charlie George fondly, because he was one of my childhood idols being from Highbury. When he signed it was incredible and I shared a room with him the night before my debut. I remember thinking '**I can't believe this, is this actually happening, what am I doing sharing with Charlie George?**' I just assumed I would have been sharing with Danny that night like we did most of the time. Of course knowing now what happened the next day, that's most probably why me and Danny weren't together and we were put with senior pros for a reason.

Training was fun, even when we had to do the fitness and running, it was still really enjoyable. Having all these experienced professionals they didn't really need coaching and the coaching staff tended to do what the players wanted. A lot of them wanted to be done before lunch so they could get to the races. It was all about man management around that time and that was how Lawrie got the best out of us all."

## AGBOOLA MOVES TO SUNDERLAND

"It was a tough move but I had to make it for my career. I was told there was no future for me at Southampton and at the time I was negotiating a new contract, so I thought there might be a chance of staying, but obviously not. I didn't really want to go but I got a call from Sunderland and I went to take a look. I made the move up north; it had its ups and downs but I don't regret it."

## RETURNING HOME

"I always get a good reception when I go back to the club. I live in Southampton and this is where I call home. The fans obviously see me a lot down here as I go to a lot of games and it's always nice to be welcomed so warmly."

# ANDY COOK

1985 - 1991
POSITION : Defender
APPS : 17
GOALS: 1

DEBUT: 15/09/1987 v Manchester United

Andy Cook's Southampton journey began as a schoolboy back in 1985 when he was spotted playing for his school team. He would work his way through the youth ranks signing pro in 1987 making is debut v Manchester United at The Dell. He would go on to play for Exeter, Swansea, Millwall, Salisbury, Woking and even had a spell at Portsmouth.

**COOKS JOURNEY BEGINS**

"I was playing football at my school, Mountbatten. My career journey really started though when a new lad came to the school called Darren Chatterley. His dad was Lew Chatterley and Lew was the first time coach at Southampton at the time. He would come and watch Darren play in the school matches. I was in the same team and that was where he saw me play and told me he would speak to the chief scout and would get me down to train at the club. I was about eleven at that stage and started training on a regular basis down at The Dell on a Wednesday evening. I was a Southampton fan growing up and all I wanted to do was be a professional footballer and play for the Saints.

I signed schoolboy forms which took me through my time at school and then at fifteen I signed as an apprentice on a two years contract. After that I was then very lucky to be offered a professional contract with the club which was incredible.

We had a strong youth set up, I was an apprentice with Francis Benali, Matt Le Tissier, and Keith Granger. The year above us we had people like Ian Hamilton, Phil Parkinson, Chris

Wilder, Craig Maskell, and Mark Blake. Then below us were Alan Shearer and Rodney and Ray Wallace. The club had a brilliant youth development system and it showed with the players that came through it."

## SIGNING PRO

"I went in to see Chris Nicholl, who was Manager at the time, in his office. I remember being sat outside waiting on tenderhooks, thinking if I was going to get contract or not. Waiting and hoping for it to be good news. At the same time I was also preparing myself just in case it was going to be bad news.

He was sat opposite me and I was just hoping for good news, hoping that he had seen enough in me to give me that professional contract and to my delight he had and there it was - my first contract.

I had not thought of trying to negotiate anything higher or better, I just saw the contract and I couldn't wait to get it signed, I was over the moon."

## THE FIRST PRE-SEASON AS A PRO

"It was incredible coming back for pre-season having only just signed my professional contract. I came back to training as a pro which was all very exciting and it was nice knowing that I now didn't have to clean four of five pairs of boots or do any of the other jobs we had to do as apprentices around The Dell.

We started pre-season training and Mark Dennis had departed the club that summer. So that left us without a recognised left back. I was a left winger but I had played a few games at fullback in the youth team and the Reserves the previous season. I didn't do too badly playing there and Chris Nicholl gave me an opportunity during pre-season to play at left back.

I played in all the pre-season friendlies and I remember we went over to Guernsey the weekend before the first game of the season to play against Matt Le Tissier's former club. We played them on the Monday evening which happened to be my eighteenth birthday. We won the game and went back to the hotel and celebrated my birthday...sensibly I might add. I had a feeling that because I started and finished that game that it was going to potentially be me who would be playing left back on the opening game of the season. I wasn't 100% sure but by the Friday I was pretty confident it was going to be me."

## THE DEBUT v MANCHESTER UNITED 1987

"Our first game of the season was against Manchester United at The Dell. I found out I was playing the day before, the squad went up on the board, as it always did, and there was my name - Andy Cook. Just six days after my eighteenth birthday I was about to make my debut.

I remember turning up to The Dell, heading into the dressing room and there it was, my number three shirt hung up ready for my debut.

There was also two letters that had been sent to me in my place, but they had been opened. I was looking around thinking **'Which cheeky sod has opened my post?'**

Then Dennis Rofe popped his head through the door said **'Andy, the letters. I did that, I opened them. You're making your debut today and I wanted to check no one had sent you anything that would have given you any negative thoughts going into the game.'** So it was Dennis who opened my letters, but for completely the right reasons. They were from no one I knew, they were from fans who wanted to give me encouragement for the game which was lovely.

Walking out at The Dell was incredible. It was the very first game of that 1987 - 1988 season and there was an air of anticipation after a long summer break. That first game always carries a little bit of magic. It was a hot August day and it was a packed house.

Running out on the pitch knowing you were making your debut against Manchester United was very special. I was playing against the likes of Bryan Robson, Gordon Strachan, Norman Whiteside and Viv Anderson who was making his debut for United that day after signing from Nottingham Forest.

I had to mark Gordon Strachan that day, so I had my hands full with him and Viv Anderson who was making overlapping runs, so it was a fun afternoon. Funnily enough I ended up nutmegging Strachan that game and then hitting the bar, so I won't tell you what he called me! We drew 2-2, Danny Wallace scored both of our goals. It was a fantastic day and it went by in a blur. I remember waking up on the Sunday morning and someone phoned me up and said **'You've made the dream team in the Sunday papers'**, so I guess I didn't play too bad that day."

### TRYING TO SECURE THE LEFT BACK SPOT

"After making my debut, I then played in the next match v Norwich away, we won that game and then next up was a game against Portsmouth at Fratton Park. Pompey had just been promoted and a former Saint, Alan Ball, was the Manager.

That week we signed Derek Statham from West Bromwich Albion, he had failed a medical at Liverpool and we then picked him up. He started that game v Portsmouth ahead of me and went on to play every game for the rest of the season and even picked Player of the Year, he was an incredible player.

Fortunately for me, I was still in and around the team, I was on the bench and travelling with the squad to games which as a young pro was brilliant.

A big problem for me was injury. I had some hamstring problems while I was at Southampton, I also had to have a back operation to have part of a disk removed and also operations on my groin. So at times it was a little bit stop-start, but every year I would make a few more appearances. In my last season, I played eleven games for the first team, but I just struggled to get a long run of fitness which would have enabled me to cement my place in the first team."

### LEAVING THE SAINTS

"It was one of those decisions I had to make, and sometimes I reflect on it and think maybe I should have stayed as I had only just signed a new three year deal under Chris Nicholl. Ian Branfoot then took over, I came back pre-season and I was struggling having just had my back operation in the summer, so wasn't really up to speed with everything. I don't know whether that affected Branfoot's judgment or if he was even aware that I had surgery, but either way he pulled me into the office and said **'Alan Ball had been on the phone, he's at Exeter and he would like to have a word with you about a move'**. I thought about it and decided that maybe this was what I needed to kick start things, a fresh challenge and then take it from there.

I remember bumping into Alan Ball as a young pro in Simon's Wine Bar a few years before. I was with my now wife and I was only just eighteen and he was at Portsmouth then. I had a really good chat with him and I remember him giving me lots of advice. He was incredibly passionate about football and his wife Lesley was a fantastic lady too.

So when this move was put on the table I went over to his house in Chandlers Ford. It was a lovely sunny summer's day and his family was all over having a barbecue in the garden. Me and my wife went and sat in the lounge with Alan and Lesley. Lesley did all the talking really, she was the one who sold the club to me, telling us what a lovely place it was. Me and Alan then discussed the finer details of the move and that was it, I had made the decision, I was leaving Southampton and going to Exeter."

### FORMER SAINT ALAN BALL AT THE HELM

"Alan was fantastic to work with at Exeter. Very infectious, very enthusiastic, wore his heart on his sleeve and was a very passionate man. He was a real player's Manager, training was great, it was fun, high tempo and he would join in now and again and he still had it. He had an incredible touch and was a real classy player. It was quite interesting at Exeter as Alan had brought in a few players that had history with either Southampton or Portsmouth. We had players like Steve Moran, Vince Hilaire, Paul Wimbledon and Steve Williams was his assistant. It was a great season and we went from third from bottom in the league to fifth from the top in what is now League One."

### PLAYING AT THE OTHER END OF THE M27

"I had two seasons at Exeter which were very enjoyable. I had just had another groin operation and a few of the players had gone. The likes of Kevin Miller and Scott Hiley had been sold and I could see the club was changing. I had offers from a few other clubs, so from there I was sold to Swansea. I had three years at Swansea and was coming to the end of a contract there.

We'd been relegated and we had been through six or seven Managers that season culminating in Jan Mølby taking over and we nearly avoided relegation. They offered me a new contract but I decided that I needed a move and for the first time ever I employed an agent.

He phoned me up one day and said '**Get yourself down to Portsmouth, I have made a call and they are expecting you**'. So I went to Stoneham Lane training ground which is where we trained when I was a Saints player and also where we train now for Eastleigh. I turned up to find Martin Hinshelwood taking the reserve team training; the first team were away on tour and no one had a clue I was turning up. So I'm not too sure that agent ever did make that call. Martin kindly let me train with them over the following few weeks.

The first team came back, they had a look at me in training, Terry Fenwick was the Manager at the time and I ended up training with them for six months before they managed to agree some sort of deal with Swansea to make the move happen. I ended signing on loan for a month initially, played five games and then only went on to play nine games for them.

As a Saints fan and former player, I thought I might escape some of the wrath having been at Exeter and Swansea in-between, but I still got quite a bit of stick. Luckily I didn't play too many times at Fratton Park."

# JOS HOOIVELD

2011 - 2015
**POSITION**: Defender
**APPS**: 67
**GOALS**: 8

**DEBUT**: 10/19/2011 v Nottingham Forest

**SAINTS HONOURS**: Championship Runner Up 2011 - 2012

Jos Hooiveld joined Southampton in the summer of 2011 from Celtic. In his first season he was an instrumental part of the defensive line in helping the Saints to secure their return to the Premier League playing alongside Jose Fonte. Scoring the third goal in the final home game of the season v Coventry, he also played his part going forward with eight goals in the 2011 - 2012 campaign. Working under three managers during his time, he was part of the squads that saw amazing progress under Nigel Adkins, Mauricio Pochettino and Ronald Koeman establishing Saints back in the top flight.

## DEADLINE DAY MOVE TO THE SAINTS

"The year before there was some interest in me from the club, so I knew all about Southampton having looked into it before, but that year I ended up moving to Celtic. My Celtic career didn't go too well and I ended up on loan at Copenhagen.

So when that interest came again from Southampton on transfer deadline day the next season, I already knew a bit about the Saints so it helped with making my decision. Crystal Palace were also in for me but because I already knew about Southampton it was an easy choice. I flew in and we landed at London City Airport, so we drove quickly down to Southampton. I met up with the Chairman who told me his story and how he approached things and what he wanted to achieve. Initially it was only a loan move for six months but after three months they took up the option to buy me."

## BECOMING PART OF THE TEAM
"It was quite easy to fit in with the squad as there was a great team there. When I joined, Danny Seaborne picked up an injury which meant they threw me straight in. It was really unfortunate for him but for me it was a flying start. I picked up pace and my first goal came in a cup game with Preston North End and then later I got another v West Ham. I had made an impression and after a few games I started hearing the fans sing **'Nigel sign him up, Nigel Nigel sign him up'** so that was a good sign that I was doing something right.

The team was just amazing, there were a lot of English guys and everybody fitted in well, we had a great group. We had one of the best atmospheres in a dressing room that I have ever been in."

## NIGEL ADKINS AND THE TEAM OF 2011 - 2012
"I loved working with Nigel. He was very rational, very down to earth, he was always looking at things to improve and was also approachable. He could be angry with you and you be angry with him but the next day you could have a laugh about it, it was very easy to get along with him.

It was a special side, when you're in the middle of it all you don't always see it that way because you're working together every day, you're playing the games and chasing the results. But when you look back on it you see what incredible quality players we had."

## PROMOTION TO THE PREMIER LEAGUE FINAL GAME OF THE SEASON v COVENTRY
"It was an amazing game. José Fonte who played alongside me scored his first of that season in that game. He scored the second and I said **'I can't let you score on your own, I need to join in'** and I made my own as well.

The best part is that people have always said that my goal was the goal that sealed promotion to the Premier League for Southampton. That was what the commentator said, so every time I show people the goal I always say '**I scored the goal that was worth a £110,000,000 that day**'.

The atmosphere was very tense, we started off really poor. I think Kelvin Davis made a few good saves to keep us in the game. It was one of those days where you were waiting for the first goal, but the longer the game went on you just couldn't see it coming. You started to think '**Oh my God this could go totally wrong**'. Luckily the goal came, Billy Sharpe got the first and then José got the second goal. That really settled the game and then of course Adam Lallana rounded it all off with the fourth.

At full time it was quite funny because I saw a lot of guys running inside to the dressing room as the fans made their way onto the pitch, and I was like '**No chance I'm missing out, I want to be part of this**'. I remember at one point Ricky Lambert was on the shoulders of the fans one side of the pitch and I was on the other. I'm sure I was upside down at one point too! It was incredible, but in the beginning it was also a little bit frightening because the fans came at you from all sides.

I couldn't move at one point, fans were trying to pull my shirt off and at one point I had to push myself a little bit to the space so I could breathe. But it was immense! You could feel the happiness from everyone that was there that day, it was so nice to see it and be part of it.

I think it's fair to say that the frustration of not being in the Premier League for all those years all came out that day. Southampton were back, it was a great day."

## HOOIVELD IN THE PREMIER LEAGUE

"For me personally as a professional footballer, to say you have played in the Premier League is really special. Looking back I remember speaking to Danny Butterfield about it and we said that the road towards the Premier League was the best bit because you were winning the games and the atmosphere built up more and more as you got closer to it. When you get to the Premier League and the media tip you for relegation, you're not playing for the title. But you were in the promise land and that was where you wanted to be.

The step up to the Premier League is also another level for you as a player, and sometimes for me that was a struggle. It was my first time there and I was already a little bit older than the other lads and coming up against the likes of Eden Hazard and Sergio Agüero that's not easy. When you look back it was an incredibly enjoyable time, but when you were in the middle of it you did think '**I enjoyed the Championship more**'. I was always fighting to keep up instead of being on my level. I became more of a squad player but it's amazing to say that I played Premier League. Nobody can take that away from me."

## THE ARRIVAL OF POCHETTINO & KOEMAN

"I really enjoyed working with both Mauricio and Ronald, because when you're in the Premier League you work with the best.

For me, Mauricio Pochettino is one of the best. He was really detailed, he was really focused and he had a great idea of the way he wanted us to play. You knew what to do when you had ball and where your options would be. Also with defending, we all knew what we had to do when we didn't have the ball. It was all laid out for you, it was an experience for me and I cherish that massively.

Ronald Koeman, now he was a hero of mine growing up. When I was about five or six Koeman was my favourite player of all time. He wore the number four so I wanted to have that number and I remember him having an incredible shot, he was brilliant to watch and he also came from the same town as me in the north of the Netherlands.

It was amazing to work with him, I was only there for a short time with him but I thought we had a great connection. The thing is with me, once I'm working with someone it's just like another person who I respect for what we are doing together. I always judge people on how they are as a person and I really liked him. Which I guess is a good thing but also sometimes I wish I was looking up to people a little bit too. He was a great coach and I had a really good three months with him."

## TEAMMATES

"One of my closest friends was always Steven Davis, I am still in touch with him and we speak regularly. I recently went to a surprise party for Danny Butterfield which was really good fun. I also got on with Kelvin Davis and Danny Fox who I still speak too and also Richard Chaplow who I played with again at Millwall. I also really cherish the time me and Rickie Lambert had together very much.

José Fonte, I met him when he played against Ajax for Lille. Maya Yoshida, I spoke with him recently. You have a real bond with a team that gets promotion together and goes through what we did. I know the whole team is still hanging out with each other and when it's possible for me, I'm also there."

## THE FANS
"The fans were great, they had a nice song about me at the start, I really enjoyed them and hopefully they enjoyed me as well for being who I am."

# LIFE OF A SAINT

## THE HOME OF A SAINT
# THE DELL
1898 - 2001

**CAPACITY:** 15,200

**RECORD ATTENDANCE:**
31,044 v Manchester United
8th October 1969

**CONSTRUCTION COST:**
£7,000 - £9,000

**INAUGURAL MATCH:**
3rd September 1898 v Brighton United

**FINAL GAMES:**
19th May 2001 v Arsenal - Premier League
26th May 2001 v Brighton & Hove Albion

The home of the Saints is currently St Mary's but for many years, and for the majority of the players in this book, their home was The Dell. So far, you will have read some of their memories of that great ground and what it meant to them, but I thought there was only one way to finish this book and that's with you, the fans. A big thank you to all of you who left a comment and also to the Saints Archive, Saints World and the Southampton Australian Supporters for sharing on their forums.

I asked the question: **"What does The Dell mean to you and what are your memories?"** and this is what you all had to say about that very special place we all called home.

**LEON BURTON:** "My fondest memory of The Dell has always got to be my very first match there at the age of ten. It was September 1965 when my dad said to me, **'I'm going to take you to The Dell to see Saints play Wolves'.** I remember walking up Hill Lane, he bought me a rosette and a programme as we entered the Milton Road end. I'd never seen so many people together in all my life. My dad had to help me push the 'boys' heavy turnstile to get me in the ground. We positioned ourselves behind the goal about halfway up the Milton Road terrace behind a crash barrier; there were no seats in those days. It seemed an age before the teams ran out from the corner of The Dell. Then at ten to three the teams appeared. Saints with their splendid red and white striped shirts and Wolves with their bright all gold strip. Being a small ten year old I could not see much so my dad hoisted me up so I could sit on the crash barrier. That was much better. I remember seeing the block of flats at the Archers Road end and wished I would live there when I grew up. Before I knew it we were a goal down in the first minute. An own goal too. It was going to be ok though because we won 9-3!"

**JULIE GREENSHIELDS:** "St Mary's is great, but can never replace The Dell in my affections. My late dad and I were regulars there from my teenage years, so it played a major part in my life, when the lasting memories were made and when the result of the Saints game was one of my few worries in life!"

**EVETS SNIKTA:** "Wonderful days, going to The Dell as a child with my dear old departed dad to watch the great Ron Davies in the 60's! I'd go back in the blink of an eye!"

**TOM SMITH:** "My dad and I had season tickets in the Family Centre in the Upper Milton. He would stand me on a box at the back of the stand and tie my scarf around my chest and around the spikes so I didn't fall off, very happy days."

**SUE TURNER:** "It was my second home. I went to every home game. I started going at 9 years old and the buzz around the ground was just the best feeling."

**PAUL STRATTON:** "My first recollection was the 1968/69 Combination Cup Final 2nd leg v West Ham United. It was a pretty big game, I recall 18,000 plus and Saints won 3-1. I remember Channon, Stokes, Judd and a couple more fringe first team players played. I was sat in the chocolate box with my dad the late Jimmy Stratton, one of the founders of the tyro league. Very happy memories indeed. Leon Crouch told me that the trophy is now at St Mary's, how superb is that."

**ROY BLAKE:** "I can remember going to one of the first floodlight games, a friendly between Saints and Bournemouth. I stood under the half time score board."

**CHRIS HOPKINS:** "I was born in Lodge road and as a nipper I can remember hearing the crowd when I was in the garden. Natural curiosity led to me to tagging on with my uncle in the mid sixties. We always went in the Archers in the corner under the scoreboard. I graduated to the Milton in my teens (with occasional visits to the Archers) and also did a stint under both West and East stands. Finally I ended up at the back of the bike shed, back row with my flag on the wall behind. It was the best of times and (rarely) the worst of times!"

**SCOTT CAMPBELL:** "My nan worked at The Dell in the players dining area with her colleague and best friend Kath. She used to cook egg and chips for Matt Le Tissier and co. Her name was Vera Campbell, she had many happy memories working there and loved every minute of it."

**EDDIE WILKINSON:** "My youth and the atmosphere!"

**WAYNE CROAD:** "Loved it there when my big bruv @Tuckerman7 and @Pinktuck who used to take me when I was a kid."

**MICHELLE TUCKER:** "My biggest memory is of Neil Ruddock being sent off against Norwich on my first visit."

**CHRIS HUTCHINGS:** "Turning up with my dad in the early 80's at 12:30pm for a 3:00pm to get a good place on the Milton Road terrace surrounded by other kids standing on milk crates to get a better view."

**CHRIS WRAGG:** "Barry Horne, 45 yarder vs Bolton and Le Tiss doing anything."

**ALAN HARRY:** "Le Tiss, Franny and relegation battles."

**IAN LAWLER:** "I like to think I served my Saints supporting apprenticeship in these hallowed stands."

**MARK COTTLE:** "Running back in when Barry Horne scored equaliser in the cup from half way line."

**JOHN LAMBERT:** "Getting there late and standing in the back and having about 8 inches of view."

**JULIAN HOOD:** "Way too many fond memories, but beating Liverpool 4-0 and the 6-3 against Man Utd ate up there. Loved the Dell."

**TOM FORDER:** "My old man dropping me down 2 rows of seats after Matt Le Tissier's last minute winner. I was 5."

**DANNK K:** "Matt Le Tissier was warming up and blasted one into the crowd and sent my drink flying."

**BARRY COOMBES:** "Watching loads of all time greats, Channon, Paine, Davies, Ball, Keegan, Shilton, Best, Moore, the Charlton's, the list goes on!"

**MARTIN MUDDIMAN:** "Amazing ground. Spent my time going most Saturdays during the 80's and 90's. The ground had a great feeling about it. Night games were extra special. I loved The Dell. My first game was with my dad in the Milton Road end when I was four years old in 1979. The ground had such an atmosphere on game day or under the lights. I stood in the family centre for years. My paper round money used to buy my entry and a programme."

**@WSmman:** "Very fond ones, my first ever game 1974, with both my grandparents and my dad. I had a season ticket through the late eighties and nineties, great atmosphere with some entertaining players and games."

**@PSIMPSON:** "Saints 9, Wolves 3 the season Wolves were relegated from the old First Division then going away to Wolves and drawing 1-1, David Webb scoring the equaliser."

**THOMAS LUFFMAN:** "Danny Wallace scoring that scissor kick against Liverpool. Kevin Keegan's disallowed goal and so many great games and players. And of course that last goal scored by probably our greatest servant Le Tiss."

**JAMIE PRAGNELL:** "My first game was on 7th April 1984, I remember walking up the steps of the Milton Road up to the Family Section with my 'fold up' step so I could see the game and all I could remember was a sea of green in front of my eyes, with Captain Sensible's 'Glad it's all over' playing over the tannoy. The match was against Leicester City, and I can't remember anything about the game other than the result. We drew 2-2 with Danny Wallace and Steve Moran scoring for Saints and Gary Lineker scoring twice for Leicester. I was also later blessed with seeing Saints beating Coventry City 8-2, with Danny Wallace and Steve Moran scoring a hat-trick each, and then beating Tottenham Hotspur 5-0 about a week later. What a fantastic introduction to going to see Southampton play, I had (and still do) collected the Panini football stickers. So to see my idols in the flesh for the first time really gave me goosebumps, and still does!"

**TREVOR PHILLIPS:** "I can't actually remember the very first time I went to The Dell but it would have been for a reserve game in the early seventies. Mum would go shopping in town while me and dad would go to the game. I think we hardly missed a match back then and Brentford Nylons' profits must have soared. I remember the crackly tannoy announcing the goals from wherever the first team were playing that day. Supporters from my era often talk about the greenness of the grass and the smoky haze from the terraces when asked about their first experience at a match. This is absolutely true in my case. My first 'proper' match was versus QPR in 1974. We sat up in the East Stand Milton Wing (row E seat 56) where my dad and his mate had season tickets. I still vividly recall walking up the creaky steps into the stand for the first time and being amazed by the sight and smell of the cigarette smoke wafting across the ground. I also remember trying to fathom out what the fans on the Milton Road terrace were singing about and thinking what a great view it must be from up in the Chocolate Boxes. To this seven year old everything seemed massive back then, but as we know The Dell even then was pretty small and cramped compared to most grounds. All the floorboards under the seats were wooden and everyone would stamp their feet in time with 'Oh When the Saints...'. It created quite a racket."

**PAUL BRENT:** "My auntie lives in Milton Road and my late dad used to put me on seat on his bike when I was about 5 and ride us from Redbridge to her house. We would meet my uncle Stan and cousin Nick and go to home games one week and reserve the next. My first game was about 1963 and my first away game was a 5-2 win at Fratton."

**NICK DUNCALFE:** "I wish we still had The Dell or even a better memorial to the place. I'd take it over St Mary's any day. The atmosphere, the nostalgia and just the proper football ground feel. My first game was a 2-2 draw against Man Utd in 1994. But one that stands out was in our final season, being 3 down to Liverpool and coming back to draw 3-3 with a certain MLT coming on the pitch and taking charge, with Pahars equalising in the last seconds."

**BRIAN SMITH:** "My first and only visit to the Dell with my father was in 1939 to see Saints against Newcastle in 0-0 draw, when I was six he sadly lost his life on HMS Hood in 1941. I started going again in 1942 and was hooked from then on. Graduated from Milton Road End to East Stand Wing. Now an exile in Birmingham but once a Saint always a Saint."

**ROBERT KEARLEY:** "First ever game at the Dell, beating Watford 4-0 in the league cup. Sadly lost 7-1 in the second leg at Vicarage Road."

**STEWART HAYTER:** "I would sum my memory of it up as a place of friendship. Met many friends at The Dell. True story I am from Taunton, when it first went all seater I was at college. Two seasons in I applied to sit near to my mates. I was two seats away and between us was a guy and his lad. We got talking one day and he asked where I was from. Turned out his company had an office in Taunton and he knew my then girlfriend (now wife) as she worked for the same company! Small world eh!"

**EDWARD SMITH:** "The Dell meant family to me. I don't come from Southampton or anywhere near, nor do I have any connections with the city but on my first visit I was welcomed like one of their own. I was hooked and have made many friends in the 50+ years since. The warmth of the people, the atmosphere created (particularly under the lights) and the togetherness created made The Dell oh so special. The Saints family are as good as it gets."

**MATT NORRIS:** "I don't really remember too much about it, a couple of things I do remember though was the home debut of Marian Pahars against Blackburn and everyone losing it when he scored late in the game. I did also get into the changing rooms at The

Dell once as well, got my shirt signed by Le God and Hassan Kachloul and gave James Beattie a picture I drew of him. I think I was maybe like 6 or 7 years old at the time. Don't remember a lot but the stuff I do remember is pretty good."

**STEVE ALLWOOD:** "Barry horn scoring a screamer from 35 yards against Bolton in an FA Cup replay the whole ground went off, pitch invasion the works, brilliant night."

**DEAN O'LEARY:** "I went to my first and only Dell match in 1985 it was the first day of the 85/86 season v Newcastle. I was on holiday in the UK at the time and I wrote to the club explaining my situation that I was a Saints supporter from Australia on holiday in the UK and a Saints supporter since 1975. I was wondering how I go about getting a ticket to the game v Newcastle as I was staying in Birmingham at the time at my aunt's place. Well a week later to my surprise I got 2 free tickets to the game sent to me. I was so excited I even forgot my camera so no photos of the day unfortunately, but the highlight of that day was when I had my name announced over the PA at half time. The result ended 1-1 a good match as well, Dave Puckett was the scorer for Saints. The atmosphere was brilliant, I'll never forget it. I've been to St Mary's also it's not the same of course, The Dell was way better on atmosphere in my opinion, but I did really enjoy my two games at St Mary's in 2017."

**DAVID HUNTER:** "My uncle was a steward and used to take me to every home game as a kid up until about 15 when I would go by myself with a mate. The only problem with going with a steward was we had to be there for 11:30 on a Saturday morning for a 3pm kickoff! Loved it though, would hang about to see the players coming into the ground. Then I'd go up to the family section for the game."

**PETER MORGAN:** "Being there when Le Tiss scored in the last game. Pint in the Pensioners or The Bedford before the games and 8-2 against Coventry."

**IAN NICHOLSON:** "100% Barry Horne's goal in cup game!"

**STUART WATSON:** "Queuing outside the Milton Road on a rainy Tuesday night to watch Man Utd for a record crowd 30,000 all standing."

**TODD WYETH:** "6-3 Against Man United!"

**BASIL BUTT:** "1976 Cup Replay v WBA, whole ground was rocking even before kick off. Saints players said the noise reached the dressing room and that's why the West Brom players looked shell shocked before they even got on the pitch!"

**STEVE WHITE:** "I loved The Dell, I stood at the Milton Road end. I was at the last game there when Le Tiss got the winner against Arsenal, good memories."

**EDDIE STICKLAND:** "Just two words THE BEST!"

**SIMON HAMPTON:** "Many many great memories over the years but the best moment has to be the Kevin Keegan's disallowed goal! The roof literally blew off! A few seconds of absolute euphoria!"

**DARREN STEVENS:** "Loved going to the Dell, stood as a teenager in the pouring rain with mates packed in but the atmosphere was always so good whatever the weather. We would score a goal and you'd celebrate like crazy, once it had died down you would look round and see all of your mates had gone missing, you'd be miles apart some how and then spend

the next few mins working your way back towards each other. You would then see somebody holding up a shoe that had been lost in the celebrations which was funny till you realised it was your shoe. Great fun times."

**TONY SHEPHERD:** "The happiest of memories from teenage years and beyond, and friendships made for life."

**AL @NewMiltonSaint:** "St Mary's has never matched the aura or atmosphere of The Dell under floodlights. Lucky to have experienced it. So many games and memories."

**ROB @EditSouthampton:** "Cold dark nights, singing non stop and loving every single moment?"

**SIMON FETTES:** "My first game was on 6th December 1975 against Sunderland. I was 9 and my dad and I were in the Milton Road end. He sat me on one of the barriers. There was a snow storm and Saints won 4-0. Then there is the sadness of the final game against Brighton and having the honour with 15,000 other people of walking on the hallowed turf."

**DAVID PILGRIM:** "Born in Milton Road and proud of it! Didn't get to show my skills on the pitch though! Shame it would have made a great story."

**IAN COX:** "Born and lived at 125 Milton Road from the age of seven. I remember queuing from ten in the morning to a great view up in the chocolate box great memories."

**BEN ANDREWS:** "My first ever game: Saints 6-3 Luton Town, I was so young I remember being disappointed that I couldn't hear any commentary! Always remember having to get in the top of the Milton End ridiculously early on match day so we could get a standing place at the front so we could actually see!! Also remember queuing for around 5 hours along Milton Road to get tickets for the Marian Pahars great escape moment!"

**PAUL LOUGHLIN:** "All my great memories are from The Dell. From the first time there in 1975 at 9 years old. It was a night game and I still remember how green the grass looked! The seasons in div2 with Phil Boyer, Ted McDougall scoring goal after goal then the wow of Keegan signing for us and even the best unbelievable moment of all time Le Tiss scoring that last minute last goal! Seems like yesterday!"

**JAMIE MATHIESON:** "Sitting at the back of The West Stand and there was cracks in the floor and you could see kitchens below and the usual stretching of your neck round a pillar to see the vital goal!"

**ANNE MACKLIN:** "Went with my dad when I was nine. Never forgot it and spent most of my teenage years walking up on a Saturday from Northam. After my girls grew up started every Saturday in The Dell Club and again afterwards. Miss that club."

**YVONNE CURTIS:** "So many brilliant memories of the Dell, My first game in October 1974, getting there at 12:30 to stand under the clock, Hughie Fisher's equaliser, us winning the

FA Cup and the magic of being at Wembley. Mick Channon's testimonial, what an atmosphere, the signing of Kevin Keegan, us finishing second 83-84 season."

**GRAHAM HILEY:** "These days the press get the best seats in the ground but the press box at the Dell was awful. It was like a chicken run, a long and very narrow wooden enclosure right at the back of the main stand. My seat (or rather a wobbly stool) was right at the far end on the right as we looked at the pitch. The view of one goal was obscured by a pillar and being at the far end meant I was the last to receive the plate of half-time sandwiches provided by the club. We were jammed shoulder to shoulder with very little workspace for a notebook and phone. In an era before laptops, match reports were dictated down the phone to a copy taker with punctuation needing to be added and all names spelled out. Occasionally the copy taker would mis-hear, which is why Saints once ended up playing Liverpool at Ampfield! It was a wonderful place to work. We witnessed some fantastic games and goals as well as the privilege of watching Matthew Le Tissier at his sublime best. It was cramped, uncomfortable and home."

**GORDON SLOAN:** "40 years of memories of the Dell. What made it so special was the atmosphere it could generate. You were so close to the pitch you almost felt part of the team. Visiting teams never looked forward to playing there even when Saints were on a poor run. I particularly remember the 5th round replay in 1976 against WBA. The teams were lined up and for some reason there was a short delay before the ref blew his whistle. The whole crowd started singing when the saints go marching in and within minutes Saints were a goal up and cruised to a 4-0 win. Sadly you couldn't replicate that atmosphere in a new ground."

**TOM BLAHA:** "I became a Saints fan in 1976 whilst on a teacher exchange from the US to Barton Peveril College in Eastleigh. My first match at The Dell was the 4-0 win over Olympique Marseille. My other great memory of The Dell, was the opening game of the 1980 season, when I came back to see Kevin Keegan's Saints debut. Arrived Gatwick at 10 a.m. that Saturday morning, and was standing in the Milton Road end at kick off time. Been a Saints fan over 40 yrs."

LIFE OF A SAINT

# THE NEXT VOLUME OF OUR HISTORY IS COMING
# RELEASED 1st MAY 2021

## #LifeOfASaint76
### WWW.LIFEOFASAINT.CO.UK

LIFE OF A SAINT